AIKIDO TO ZEN

AIKIDO TO ZEN

The Story of Martial Arts

Jules Stewart

REAKTION BOOKS

To Grandmaster Donato Nardizzi

Published by
REAKTION BOOKS LTD
2–4 Sebastian Street
London EC1V 0HE, UK
www.reaktionbooks.co.uk

First published 2026

EU GPSR Authorised Representative
Logos Europe, 9 rue Nicolas Poussin, 17000, La Rochelle, France
email: contact@logoseurope.eu

Printed and bound in Great Britain by Bell & Bain, Glasgow

A catalogue record for this book is available from the British Library

ISBN 978 1 83639 257 6

CONTENTS

Shi Yan Gui, headmaster at Shaolin Temple
Martial Arts and Cultural Centre, London.

FOREWORD
BY MASTER SHI YAN GUI

To be a martial artist means something different to each of us, but the passion we share comes from the same place. Martial arts is about self-improvement. It transcends the challenges of modern life, offering solutions for both physical and mental health. It helps us cultivate a deeper connection with ourselves, creating a sense of inner peace that goes beyond the survival-based origins of combat. Martial arts inspires compassion, confidence, respect and calmness. The discipline it teaches forms an unbreakable connection with ourselves and a profound understanding of the human condition.

Whether we're practising, teaching or simply watching, martial arts excites us and ignites feelings of inspiration and resilience. It pushes us to never give up, empowering us to face life's challenges. It brings people together, sparking viewers' excitement when it's shown on screen, our own joy when we practise ourselves or when we see someone else improving, beginning their journey or being inspired. Martial arts has roots and traditions that stretch across the world. There are countless martial arts styles, but no matter the style practised, its practitioners all share an unwritten code: martial arts isn't for hurting others. It's for improving ourselves, defending ourselves and to inspire personal growth.

Today, martial arts is not just a combat art but a widely practised sport and hobby. Millions of people across the globe, from all walks of life, embrace it. It has become something for everyone, providing physical, mental and cultural benefits. It brings harmony between the body and mind, and it's open to people of all ages and abilities.

For many, martial arts is essential for the human spirit. It's a lifeline, a form of expression, a way of life and a means of personal transformation. In my own life, martial arts transformed me, just as it has for many others, especially refugees and asylum seekers like myself. Martial arts is a celebrated sport in Europe, a powerful tool for building community and celebrating skill. In China and much of Asia, martial arts holds a place of immense cultural value, and this is something I've personally come to appreciate after exploring various styles throughout my youth in Iran. Growing up in Iran, combat was a necessity. Fighting in the streets or through competitions was the norm. Yet martial arts showed me a different way of fighting, one that's focused on peace, balance and inner calmness. After practising many styles, I found solace in Chinese martial arts and its philosophy, particularly Wushu.

In traditional Chinese culture, Wushu is much more than just a fighting style. It encompasses a vast array of practices with deep, diverse characteristics. Shaolin kung fu, one of the most ancient and most revered styles, is rooted in Chan (Zen) Buddhism. However, without understanding the deeper philosophical aspects of Chan and the Shaolin culture, Shaolin kung fu practice is incomplete. The Shaolin Temple is undeniably the birthplace of Shaolin kung fu and from there it spread around the world. It has been depicted in a multitude of films and has become a symbol of martial arts culture, largely due to the leadership of my master, the Venerable Abbot Shi Yongxin, whose countless efforts to spread the Chan culture opened the temple to the world. Today, the Shaolin Temple is recognized as a place of national intangible cultural heritage and has also been designated a UNESCO World Heritage Site.

Through centuries of practice, the Shaolin Temple has nurtured a long lineage of martial artists, and I am proud to be a 34th-generation secular disciple. It is from Shaolin that many martial artists across China and the world have drawn inspiration, each developing their own methods and styles.

The Shaolin Temple was and is a sanctuary for people in need of transformation. It offers refuge and healing through martial arts and the teachings of Chan Buddhism. One of the most iconic weapons of Shaolin kung fu is the staff, known as the *Gun*. This wooden weapon was designed for defence, not for causing harm. It represents the Shaolin philosophy of protection, not destruction.

Many students, like myself, turned to martial arts to find healing, strength and purpose. I didn't choose martial arts as an adult, it chose me at the age of three. But the Shaolin Temple called me when I was

Kung fu monk, Shaolin Temple, China.

a young refugee in London, struggling through a difficult transition into adulthood on my own. Shaolin kung fu's enlightening philosophy helped me. This is the reason why we also sponsor and help people in need when they can't afford to attend martial arts classes at my school in London. We make the teachings accessible, as all schools should, to those who are otherwise unable to participate. I have seen transformations in numerous students who came to me broken, lost or caught in difficult life circumstances. Through Wushu and the principles of Chinese martial arts, these people were healed physically, mentally and spiritually. Martial arts is as much a game of the mind as it is a physical practice. It requires patience, discipline and a commitment to constant self-improvement.

Unfortunately, I also see many people give up on martial arts early on, unable to see past the struggles of the initial stages. They don't realize that these early challenges are vital to the mental and physical transformations that will come later. Martial arts is not just about learning combat skills. It is about lifelong study, growth and self-discovery.

Chinese martial arts, including Shaolin, Bagua, Xingyi, Taiji, Wudang and many more, are unique because they blend art, sport and philosophy. They are deeply rooted in centuries of tradition and reflect the resilience of a culture that fought to preserve its heritage. Only in recent years has the rest of the world had greater access to Chinese martial arts. The global popularity of Bruce Lee played a crucial role in this, helping to introduce kung fu to audiences in the United States and Europe. His classes brought together students from diverse martial arts backgrounds, and his legacy continues to inspire martial artists today.

I have also observed the rise of online martial arts training, which, while useful for understanding techniques, can be detrimental to beginners. The fundamentals of martial arts must be learned in person, under the guidance of an experienced teacher. Without a strong foundation, students may rush through early stages of learning, losing out on crucial lessons in discipline, patience and technique. Martial arts is about more than just physical movements. It is about cultivating a mindset of respect, patience and perseverance. These core values are only truly absorbed through in-person training.

When I first moved to London, I didn't speak English and my teachers didn't speak the same language as me. But we communicated through the universal language of martial arts. The discipline I learned in Iran, where we didn't question our teachers, helped me to focus and respect the process. Language was never a barrier, as the teachings were transmitted through actions and the heart.

Martial arts is a journey of constant adaptation and growth. Whether you're practising a traditional style like Shaolin or exploring something new, the key is to keep moving forward. Challenge yourself, keep growing and never stop learning. Through hard work and persistence, you can transform yourself physically, mentally and emotionally. The journey of a martial artist is often described as the hero's voyage. We all start with a goal: strength, fitness, self-defence or perhaps to join a community. But the transformation is not easy. It requires enduring hardship, shedding old habits and pushing through the grind. It's not a pretty process, but it's one that challenges you, shapes you and ultimately changes you for the better.

Martial arts requires the same level of commitment as other high-level sports. Whether you're training for swimming, gymnastics or football, the dedication required in martial arts is no different. Your body must become martial. Your mind must be calm and focused and your heart must remain open. It is a way of life that demands consistency, balance and energy. Martial arts is always there for you, whether you're feeling calm or facing difficult times. But it needs you to stay present, to commit to the process and to honour the tradition.

THIS BOOK IS FOR ANYONE who wants to learn more about the rich history of martial arts. Whether you're an experienced practitioner or someone new to the world of martial arts, I encourage you to keep an open mind as you explore its depths. Martial arts is a beautiful blend of mind, body and spirit, and I hope this book will help you to understand and appreciate its many facets.

With exemplary patience, practice and never giving up, the author of this book earned his black belt in taekwon-do at the age of eighty. Through his journey of understanding the universal aspects of martial arts, he has compiled this narrative for us. This book is for everyone who wants to not only explore the rich culture of martial arts around the world and martial arts' history but to gain a theoretical understanding of its beginnings. It offers knowledge and insight into thorough research that will surprise you, exploring traditions you might not have heard of before.

I hope you enjoy this book and keep an open mind to learn about the many wonderful and varied martial arts styles, teachers and masters who have left us their legacy, no matter what style of martial arts you practise and wherever you are in your life right now.

The world of martial arts is a wonderful world of transformation. Let's begin.

INTRODUCTION

It is in a sparring session that you come to understand why taekwon-do is called a martial *art*. Your gaze must remain fixed on your opponent's face, which will indicate his or her plan of attack. The temptation to watch for signals from hands or feet can bring unexpected and painful consequences. At the same time, you need to instantly decide your defence and counter-attack. These thoughts raced through my mind when sparring with my instructor, Alex Nardizzi, a 6th Dan (level) former British and European champion. Unfortunately, his thoughts were well ahead of mine, so no prizes for guessing who won.

Nevertheless, a few weeks short of my eightieth birthday it was agreed I had 'the potential' to grade for my black belt in taekwon-do. Still, concerned about the age issue, I asked my GP for guidance on what I planned to do. 'Hmm,' she frowned, 'you can probably expect to sustain injuries if you tangle with any twenty-year-olds. Needless to say, you may also be risking a heart attack.'

I spoke with a friend whose judgement I trust and put the question to him over tea. He steepled his fingers and asked if I was prepared to put myself in danger of serious bodily damage, in what he kindly referred to as my 'declining years'.

I sought counsel from a veteran martial arts practitioner. 'I think this is perhaps not a good idea, you know, because of your age,' he said, stroking his venerable white beard. 'You may be wasting your money on the grading fee.'

Contrary to my GP's opinion, my instructor expressed confidence that I was trained well enough to endure the test, so one drizzly Saturday morning found me sharing a *dojang* in East Croydon with a roomful of outrageously fit twenty-something-year-olds. *This is it*, I told myself, *it's now or never, the last chance saloon*. I was about to grade for my black belt in taekwon-do.

A 9th Dan grandmaster, Donato Nardizzi, one of an elite of some fifty taekwon-do instructors worldwide to bear that title and the father of my instructor, Alex, was seated behind a table at the front of the room. On his signal, we were called up to perform a sequence of kicks – turning, forward, side, hooking, reverse – up and down the sports hall. Then we were told to repeat the procedure. Finally

Former taekwon-do European champion 6th Dan Alex Nardizzi (left) practising one-step sparring with the author.

came the patterns, nine in all for a black belt aspirant, ranging from 19 to 38 movements each.

Board breaking was next on the agenda for the day's activities. This entails smashing a half-inch-thick board with a side or turning kick and breaking a second one with a punch or a strike with the side of the hand. I chose the side kick for the former, and for the latter the knife-hand strike, reasoning that a fractured wrist would be less troublesome than a set of shattered knuckles. The splintering sound that followed my two attacks was most gratifying, coming as it did from the demolished boards and not my anatomy. Finally, the heavy business of the day. Free sparring, first one-on-one and then fighting two opponents simultaneously. To top it off, we engaged in release techniques for neck chokes, headlocks and the like, always ensuring that once freed from his or her grip, your opponent is put out of action with a kick or a punch.

The final item on the agenda was the dreaded theory test. Hands up everyone who knows what *sonkal nopunde ap taerigi* means. I was summoned to the table and asked, 'Who is the pattern Choong Moo named after?' Oh glory, that was one I *did* know. 'Admiral Yi Sun Soon-Sin!' I cried out. 'He was credited with designing the *kobukson*, the world's first armoured battleship. The admiral was killed in a naval battle with the Japanese in 1598 by a stray arquebus bullet to his left side, which is why we end this pattern with a left-hand strike, to symbolize his untimely death.' Phew. Was that it? Sadly not. 'What is the Korean for elbow, fist, walking stance, reverse knife-hand front strike?' ... And so on, for another gruelling ten minutes before I was dismissed. I bowed, took three steps back, bowed again, turned and slumped onto the bench.

After this three-hour-plus ordeal, I limped home to soak in a hot bath spiked with Neal's Yard lavender oil, followed by a rubdown in the relevant spots with extra strength Tiger Balm. I took the ice pack out of the fridge, pulled on my Dr Scholl's knee braces and Vulkan neoprene lumbar support and collapsed on the sofa, trussed up like a Christmas turkey.

In Spain, where I lived for many years, it was commonly said that the day of your First Communion marked the happiest moment in your life. For me, it was the Monday morning after my grading, when I opened an email from Grandmaster Nardizzi. 'Dear Jules, I am pleased to inform you that you were successful in passing to 1st Degree.'

My age has never once been questioned by fellow students. On the contrary, I have been treated with the reverence inherent in the martial art's first tenet: courtesy. I would recommend taekwon-do to any fit pensioner. Putting your feet up is good for the circulation – delivering a turning kick is even better.

1

WHAT ARE MARTIAL ARTS?

Words of wisdom: 'If you are confronted with violence, walk away. Just don't stick your hands in your pockets.'

LATE GRANDMASTER KIM JAE WON
Taekwon-do instructor

It began in a cave. In 1933 a team of French archaeologists exploring the lunar landscape of Tassili n'Ajjer, deep in the Algerian Sahara, came across a remarkable find. In that region's ghostly rock city of Sefar they uncovered a 7,000-year-old cave painting depicting two bands of Bronze Age adversaries armed with bow and arrows and spears, engaged in ferocious combat. This discovery stands as one of the earliest graphic portrayals of human warfare.

The Neolithic Age indeed marked the dawn of sophisticated weaponry. In 2024 and some 2,400 kilometres (1,500 mi.) north across the Mediterranean Sea, a team of Spanish archaeologists from the University of Barcelona was exploring Los Murciélagos de Albuñol cave near the city of Granada. In their dig they came across a collection of bow strings. These well-preserved artefacts, believed to be the oldest discovered in Europe, were fabricated from the flesh of different species of animals. Arrows were found on the same underground site, made of sugar cane and wood from olive trees. The scientists believe that apart from hunting animals for food, the weapons were used to fight off rival human predators.

Was it a battle for supremacy between rival clans? Were these cave dwellers warring over territorial rights, hunting grounds, dominion over water resources or crop-land? More intriguingly, at least for the purposes of this narrative, is the question of whether this was a display of rudimentary martial arts in action. The less-than-helpful answer would be: yes and no.

Do the slate etchings recently unearthed, once again in south-western Spain, shed more light on this question? In 2024, after a decade of research at a dig in Casas del Turuñuelo, a fifth century BCE site in Badajoz province, a team of archaeologists came upon a stone tablet that depicts three Tartessian combatants embroiled in a clash. This time the fighters were turned out in battle dress and brandishing swords. The Tartessians were an ancient people who inhabited Spain from roughly the eighth to the fourth centuries BCE, before mysteriously vanishing from the peninsula. They are believed to have been a mixture of indigenous tribesmen and Phoenician settlers. The carvings were etched into the tablet more than 4,000 years after the Tassili n'Ajjer drawings were painted on the cave walls. From the fragments that survive in the Spanish image, the soldiers appear better disciplined and are acting more along recognizable military lines than the stormy free-for-all fighters of the Algerian paintings.

Examples from Antiquity portraying humans engaged in warfare are to be found in many other parts of the world. A notable example are the 5,500-year-old battle images engraved on the Egyptian pyramids. Entering the semi-legendary realm, there is also the work of the more contemporary Indian Buddhist monk Bodhidharma.

Two grandmasters of the Shaolin Temple: Shi DeRu (Shawn Xiangyang Liu) and Shi DeYang (Shi WanFeng), two descendent disciples of the late great-grandmaster of the Shaolin Temple Shi SuXi (aka His Holiness Upper Su and Lower Xi).

On his wanderings in the fifth century CE, Bodhidharma was said to have developed an innovative style of fighting for the friars of China's Shaolin Monastery, also known as Shaolin Temple.

What are we looking at in these drawing and carvings that span thousands of years of human existence? It is obvious that from the primeval era, the *Homo sapiens* who displaced the Neanderthals and eventually became us have consistently resorted to violence as a means of resolving their disputes. Open-handed struggle gradually gave way to the use of armaments, from stone hatchets and bladed tools to the more advanced bow and arrow, which reduced the risks of personal contact between combatants. When considering if these could be defined as early manifestations of martial arts, the 'yes' would be in the first half of the phrase. In each instance adversaries are performing a soldier-like and therefore a 'martial' feat.

This brings up the thornier conundrum of why the martial arts have earned the sobriquet of *art*, as opposed to skill, method or practice. It could be argued that these three latter terms are merely variants of 'art', but it is obvious that the word *art*, when applied to a physical pursuit, can be considered a multidimensional concept. Expressed in simpler terms, a sparring session in karate, taekwon-do or kung fu, to name but three of the scores of the recognized schools of martial arts, requires the simultaneous deployment of psychological intuition, rapid physical reaction and mental awareness.

What can we say about other forms of combat, sumo wrestling or boxing, for instance? Can they be accurately described as martial arts? To be sure, both these activities tick several of the boxes. Traditional Japanese wrestling is thoroughly regulated by the Sumo Association. Mental as well as muscle training are built in training sanctuaries, where most wrestlers spend their lives in an almost monastic environment. Hence mental alertness and bodily strength are without doubt two key elements of the sumo wrestler's performance in the ring.

The allure of sumo is spreading outside its traditional Japanese homeland. Sumo wrestlers now meet every week in Iver Heath, a village near London's Heathrow Airport. In October 2025 the Royal Albert Hall was host to more than forty Japanese sumo wrestlers, who competed in a five-day event complete with an authentic soil-and-sand ring and a roof reminiscent of a Shinto shrine. Steve Pateman, chairman of the British Sumo Federation, believes the number of British participants in sumo will take off 'once the big guys come over from Japan'.[1] UK champion Mandeep Singh Kunda is training his ten-year-old son Ash in the art. He hopes to see more people get involved, including women. 'Unlike in Japan, women are allowed to compete in the UK,' he says. 'There are some formidable female British sumo wrestlers.'[2]

BOXING CALLS ITSELF THE NOBLE ART, while wrestling and judo/jujitsu are not a million miles apart in their fighting styles. It is difficult to identify radical differences between judo and jujitsu. Both are based on throws and strikes, and while the former places emphasis on throwing rather than punching and kicking, the latter is more focused on submission holds and holding a dominant position in combat. Judo, known as 'the gentle way', in fact originated as an offshoot of jujitsu and was founded in 1882 by Jigoro Kano, a major figure in Japanese academia and politics. Kano originally called it Kodokan Judo and the martial art was always intended to be more than just a sport. The three fundamental tenets of judo are described as physical education, contest proficiency and mental training with the ultimate goal of making the individual a value to society. This is inherent in its origins, for Kano intended judo to be a learning pursuit, as reflected in his belief that only through education can people achieve a state of happiness. The objective is to help people develop a sense of respect for the principles of maximum efficiency, well-being and mutual benefits by developing the body and learning the art of attack and defence.

'In a Judo class, students need to be totally concentrated on what they are doing and focus all their attention on what they are trying to achieve,' says Carlos Gutiérrez García, professor in the physical education faculty at Spain's University of León. 'But this is not enough. They must apply the principle of *seiryoku zen'yo*, which means their energy must be used efficiently and that students should be capable of deploying the least amount of energy to achieve their objective. This can only be attained through repeated and conscientious training.'[3]

Very little has changed with judo since its founding, apart from the introduction of weight categories and the extension of the sport to include the participation of children. What judo and jujitsu

Jigoro Kano, Japanese founder of judo, before 1938.

indisputably have in common, unlike boxing and wrestling, is that they both can call themselves true martial arts. Not a few boxing enthusiasts would assert quite forcefully that their cherished 'noble art' falls squarely within the category of a martial art. They point to the fact that boxing, practised in almost every country in the world, uses specific and systematic skills, no different from kung fu or jujitsu. It focuses on attack and defence and has a syllabus that lays out prescribed techniques and tactics. The argument goes that boxing, like any school of martial arts, makes use of a system of drills adopted for combat.

There is a persuasive counter-argument, according to which boxing is in essence a sport. 'A sport may also have techniques and forms but the aim is to win,' says taekwon-do instructor Keiron Henderson.

> A martial art is performed for itself – you can't *win* in karate, for instance. Be that as it may, almost all the best-known martial arts, apart from aikido and tai chi, embrace sparring and competition because it is human nature to compete with one another. However, a boxer or sumo wrestler eventually retires, while a martial artist does not. He or she continues to study and train.[4]

It might be added that wrestling and boxing lack the spiritual component that makes up the lifeblood of the conventional martial arts.

Sensei (Teacher) Nicolas Antoine, founder of the Ryu Kai Academy in London, agrees that pure boxing cannot be classed as a genuine martial art. 'This is chiefly due to the absence of a martial discipline,' he says. 'It is more of a free-style pursuit, lacking a strict code of ethics.' Antoine says that kickboxing does respond to the description and that he has brought together American-style boxing with the schools of Thai kickboxing and Wado Ryu, one of the four major styles of karate, to create a discipline that fully corresponds to the principles of a martial art. 'It combines kickboxing, in the use of knees, elbows and shins, as well as grappling techniques,' he says. 'Fist work is taken from American boxing and straight-forward kicking from Wado karate.'[5]

Nevertheless, the belief that kickboxing ranks as an authentic martial art is overshadowed by a degree of ambiguity. This is where opponents put on a pair of sparring gloves and step into the ring to execute a style of fighting that is karate minus its philosophy, with virtually unrestrained punching. It is a relatively new discipline, originating in Japan in the 1960s, an activity in which East meets West. It is basically a no-holds-barred fighting skill, allowing punches and kicks to any part of the body, with a ritualistic methodology. In this sense, one label for kickboxing that might effectively placate the yea- as well as the nay-sayers would be 'hybrid martial art'.

When Henderson makes mention of aikido and tai chi, he emphasizes that both prioritize spiritual and physical development over combat instruction. Aikido practitioners are indeed trained in locking and throwing techniques and, one must concede, are capable of looking after themselves when confronted with physical aggression. There is also a strong element of secretiveness in this art, handed down from its founder, the twentieth-century Japanese spiritualist and former soldier Morihei Ueshiba, who claimed to possess miraculous powers, famously among which was his alleged and somewhat arguable ability to dodge bullets.

John Corcoran, author and literary authority on martial arts, holds aikido to be the most spiritual of all the combat practices. Morihei Ueshiba was a deeply spiritual individual as well as a devoted follower of Shinto, Japan's oldest sacred faith, along with Buddhism. As a young man, Ueshiba was a practitioner of several martial arts. He took these skills with him when he served in the Japanese Army, and after the Russo-Japanese War (1904–5) he eventually moved to Tokyo, where he founded the Aikikai Hombu Dojo in 1931 (originally named Kobukan Dojo, it was renamed Hombu after the Second World War). He gained acclaim as an instructor in this dojo and in Japan's top military academies.

The most widely accepted definition of aikido is that of a practice imbued with a unifying spirit and harmony. 'It has links with Zen as well as Shinto, the national faith of Japan, both of which are synthesized into aikido practice to develop a healthy mind and body, together with a wholesome spirit,' says Corcoran.[6] Japan's religious faith is embodied in Shinto, which focuses on the worship of kami, meaning the spiritual elements of nature and humans. For this reason, aikido seeks a peaceful and centred state of mind, ideally in a setting of non-violent conflict resolution. Aikido students are easily distinguishable by their classroom dress. Their attire consists of a *hakama*, a billowing black skirt, the same as was worn by the ancient samurai. Classes require ample space to allow the *Aikido-da* (practitioner) to execute the distinctive circular movements intended to take control of an adversary's momentum by sending an aggressor hurtling to the floor on a centre axis. In synthesis, the basic concept is to exploit an opponent's energy.

Aikido training may appear to be of a softer nature than other martial arts, but this is a deceptive observation, says Greet Angèle de Baets, a lecturer at Ghent University and aikido specialist. Gathering opinions from a score of aikido experts worldwide, she explains that one of the reasons aikido training often seems undemanding is that it is not based on the reality of this practice. 'If we trained as if it were real, we could die,' she says. She quotes an expert, who explains that 'aikido seeks to resolve attacks, stop disputes and place the other party under control without inflicting any harm. This is not passive avoidance or inaction.' On the contrary, aikido 'prepares you to deal with several attackers at once, teaches you to avoid injury and is efficient'.[7]

Focusing solely on the external aspects of aikido, such as physical prowess and self-defence, hinders personal growth while directing one's awareness inward fosters development. Aikido, being a *do*, or path, requires constant refinement and polishing, emphasizing the importance of ongoing personal development. 'Aikido represents the ultimate path of lifelong learning, not merely accumulating experience or knowledge but a continuous process of self-discovery leading to a fuller understanding of oneself,' says Angèle de Baets.

> A fundamental principle central to the proper execution and fluidity of aikido [is] recognizing that one's movements extend beyond mere individual actions and instead incorporate an inseparable connection with the surrounding environment. This encompasses the physical realm, including opponents and immediate surroundings, and the broader context of society, nature, and the cosmos.[8]

The gentle, low-impact Chinese tai chi, a form of exercise infused with Taoist and Confucian thought, is practised by some 300 million people worldwide. Alternatively known as Taijiquan, tai chi is instilled with Chinese philosophical tradition and requires the student to create a spirit of harmony with the Tao, best understood as the path or method. Tai chi followers perform a series of rhythmic flowing motions while focusing on deep, slow breaths, often referred to as meditation in motion. In China it has been known under several names, such as touch boxing, soft neutralizing boxing and long boxing. Tai chi traces its origins back to tenth-century China, while more recently it has come to signify the highest force behind all reality.

'Practitioners East and West have been polarized by the issue of whether Taijiquan is essentially a fighting art or a moving meditation,' says Douglas Wile, professor of Chinese language and literature.

> Some are deadly serious about taiji as a fighting art, and some feel that taiji to fighting is what dance is in a way to sex: ways

Tai chi hand position.

to play with aggressive or erotic energy without going over the top. The Daoist-Taiji connection in China was painstakingly constructed and fiercely contested but presented to the West as a *fait accompli*.[9]

In synthesis, the definition of what constitutes a martial art is implicit in the name: this is the learning of military tactics executed with artistic skill. These are fighting arts, created for combat between two or more opponents. The history of martial arts is in essence a chronicle of conflict, a primary component of aggressive human behaviour since the appearance of genus *Homo* nearly 3 million years ago. 'At some point in man's evolution, his primal rage compelled him to climb out of the trees, pick up stones and take a stand against the animals that had been hunting him for so long,' says historian and martial arts practitioner Michael Rosenbaum. 'From this rage the art of fighting was born. This inner rage of our ancestors would

Contemporary samurai warrior illustration.

become the foundation from which many classical and contemporary martial arts and styles and systems were built upon.'[10]

In Japan, the battle-trained bushi were the noblest and from their ranks came the samurai. This brought the introduction of weapons, such as the staff, the nunchaku (a fighting tool made up of two sticks connected by a short chain or rope) and in the case of kendo, the bamboo sword. Other schools, like the aforesaid jujitsu and aikido, along with Korean taekwon-do, remained focused on the exposed body, using speed, muscle power and, if need be, a range of complex procedures to disarm an attacker. It is worth pointing out that in the public perception of martial arts, they involve the wearing of a uniform and a belt ranging in colours from white and progressing to black, the symbol of maximum proficiency.

Most crucially, the root philosophy ingrained in the teaching of martial arts is the principle that violence, whenever possible, is to be rigorously avoided. 'If you are confronted with aggression and can walk away, turn your back and walk away,' was the advice taught by a Korean grandmaster. 'But always remember not to stick your hands in your pockets.'[11] Wrestling and boxing would not exist as sports were not their aim to inflict the greatest possible damage on an opponent. In martial arts the message is self-control, particularly for those who have risen to the higher grades in their chosen field.

The 'art' in kung fu, jujitsu and the other recognized schools resides in the way the various disciplines put their techniques into action. But it is also to be found in the non-use of fists and feet in subduing an adversary. A confident look, a gesture or even an act of psychological manipulation can provide the winning firepower.

A case in point, told to me many years ago by a fellow taekwon-do practitioner: a taekwon-do grandmaster was seated in the back of a bus in Toronto when angry shouting suddenly broke out by the front entrance. A hopelessly drunk man was trying to board without paying. The female driver told him the bus would not move unless he paid his fare. At that moment, the drunkard raised a fist and began threatening the woman. The grandmaster instinctively alighted, ran to the open door and taunted the drunk until he stumbled off the bus to take up what he saw as a red cape being waved in front of his face. The grandmaster began dodging from side to side to confuse his opponent. He then quickly jumped back on the bus and told the driver to shut the doors and take off. When he returned to his seat he asked himself, *did I just use my taekwon-do?* The answer that immediately came to mind was, *Yes. I think I did.* This incident illustrates the message that martial arts students are taught in our habitually belligerent world: physical force must be used only as a last resort.

There is a very sound reason why an accomplished martial artist should exert utmost constraint in a confrontation, for the odds are that the attacker as well as the defender will end up on the losing end. One evening, a karate black belt was escorting his fiancée home from the cinema. As they turned the corner, he spotted a thief attempting to break into his car, parked in front of the woman's house. He gave a shout and began racing towards the robber, who turned and pulled out a 'zombie' knife, a fiendish tool with cutting and serrated edges. This was not a time for half-measures. The karate expert reacted instinctively. He smashed into the knife-wielder with a flying sidekick. The blow sent him tumbling backwards against the car chassis and left him with spinal fractures. This incident took place in Madrid, where a police presence is rarely far away. Both men were detained on the spot, an ambulance was called and the thief was taken to hospital, having sustained what were diagnosed as life-changing injuries. He later brought charges against his attacker. The outcome, which some might consider a perverse interpretation of justice, resulted in the defendant being obliged to pay substantial damages for what the magistrate ruled had been excessive use of force.

IT WOULD BE POINTLESS to try to determine the exact date on which a huge asteroid impact caused the extinction of Earth's dinosaur population. All we know with any degree of certainty is this cataclysmic event occurred more than 60 million years ago. Determining the date of the asteroid collision would add nothing of scientific value to the study of the more than eight hundred known species of dinosaurs. Likewise, we can only speculate on the moment in history that marked the appearance of the first of what we would identify as a true martial art. To seek answers for both incidents would amount to a futile waste of research time. With regard to the second historical event, this has not discouraged a host of historians from engaging in something resembling mortal combat to expound their theories on the birth of the martial arts in time and place. The countries that most commonly fuel this animated debate are China and Japan.

Folklore has it that sometime in the early sixth century CE the Indian monk Bodhidharma, while on a spiritual pilgrimage across Asia, came to reside at the Shaolin Temple in what is now China's Henan Province. It was at this sacred spot, his devotees insist, that the mystic monk developed a school of fighting that for the general public has come to embody a byword for martial arts: namely, kung fu. The tales of Bodhidharma's sojourn at Shaolin are sprinkled with a colourful coating of fantasy. It is claimed that the Indian monk devised kung fu to provide the monks with a sense of self-confidence, to protect themselves from marauders and also to improve their state of health. This is a Chinese expression, made up of two words that can be interpreted as meaning 'merit' (*Kung*) and 'way' and 'method' (*Fu*). The story goes that it took him nine years of intensive meditation in a nearby cave to develop this plan. This lies alongside another legend, which alleges that kung fu was a means of self-defence for Bodhidharma himself, who had to deal with savage beasts stalking the cave in which he reposed in meditation.

Historical speculation aside, the fact is that over the centuries, kung fu has developed into one of the deadliest and most mysterious of martial arts. It was and, to a certain extent, is still believed by many kung fu practitioners that if the body is struck at a certain time of day, in some vital area of the body and in a certain manner, a chain reaction will start. The attacker strikes, the victim feels no immediate effect and believes himself to be unharmed. In a few days or weeks, the victim dies or becomes seriously ill. It is not an uncommon outcome.

'Another lethal practice in kung fu is a specialised technique known as iron palm,' explains historian Peter Lewis.

> The practitioner can single with a single blow. The entire forearm must be conditioned over a period of several years. Training for this technique involves punching bags filled with sand, then later with pebbles and finally with iron fillings or metal shot. To aid a student of iron palm in the build-up of hand conditioning, a special ointment called *da jow* is used. It is said to help prevent bruising and internal injuries, while at the same time strengthening the skin, muscle and bone. No iron palm practitioner would attempt to train without first using this ointment.[12]

Guided by the teachings of Bodhidharma, who claimed to be a direct descendant of the Buddha, the monastery, nestled on the barren slopes of Song Mountain, was to become the birthplace of Zen Buddhism. With its focus on self-discipline and oneness, Zen exemplified the ideal code of ethics for those whose lives were bound to bushido. Zen's emphasis on austerity and inner salvation formed a suitable framework for the battlefield code of conduct. Bodhidharma is thus deemed to be the patriarch of this spiritual tradition, known as Chan in China and, following its migration to Japan, Zen Buddhism. This code of conduct has had over the centuries a profound impact on the teaching of martial arts in Japan, from kendo and judo to kyudo and, of course, karate.

Few, if any, physical endeavours have generated such debate as the dispute over the origins of martial arts. The Shaolin Temple is a classic case in point, and this is mainly with regard to its role as the birthplace of several schools of fighting, as well as the position of Bodhidharma in developing their guiding philosophy. 'Many popular origin narratives have positioned the Shaolin Temple as the singular origin of all Asian martial arts,' writes cultural historian Paul Bowman.

> This idea has been amply interrogated by others. Interestingly, there is a flaw in both the structure of the myth and in the face of historical evidence. That flaw relates to the fact that the mythic founder of Shaolin, Bodhidharma, came from India, and historians have argued that India has an older martial art than Shaolin. This has led some to suggest that Bodhidharma brought with him the older and more original martial art of Kalarippayattu [a twelfth-century Indian martial art said to have originated in Kerala]. Most advocates of such an idea have vested interests in promoting modern schools and forms

> of Indian martial arts and culture. This fact alone sheds some light on the motivations behind the promotion of such stories. Put bluntly, all such narratives are based on and promote certain fantasies and desires, investments that are often ethnonationalistic.[13]

Mark Li, an instructor in the Chi Body method of awareness and internal energy development, supports the hypothesis that martial arts can trace their origin to the kung fu tradition that first saw life in China. 'It has been shaped by two schools,' he says. 'The first is a religious influence, namely Buddhism, which was adapted by the Shaolin Monastery monks to their martial arts styles. The philosophical school was Daoism, which emphasizes living in harmony with the natural world order.'[14]

Li was born into what he defines as the authentic tradition of Chinese internal arts and Daoist energy cultivation. Simply put, these are practices concerned with spiritual and mental aspects, unlike the external arts that focus on physiological matters. He says that through direct transmission from his father and grandfather, he inherited the lineage, knowledge and wisdom of his predecessors, passed down over several centuries. Li began his formal contact with martial arts in his early teens, when his father took his family from Beijing to live in the United States. His training began young with his father, Grandmaster Li Tai Liang. 'At first I helped dad with his martial arts classes in New York,' he says. 'This included Chinese Kickboxing and Wushu, which resembles performance martial arts.' Li today combines his Eastern roots with a Western application. Chi Body is the method he developed for teaching what he describes as 'authentic and often secretive techniques transformed into the power of a physically aligned and healthy body, and a focused and calm mind and inner peace'. This was based on Li Tai Liang's teachings of Xin Yidao, which translates as 'the way of heart centre attention'. Li holds the position of vice-president of the World Fighting Martial Arts Federation (WFMAF), a New York-based international organization whose mission is to preserve the original martial root of martial arts through communication, exchange and research. He maintains that over the past several decades, internal arts and energetic practices have rapidly spread from East to West. Daoist meditation, qigong and tai chi have become popular, with tens of millions of practitioners around the world today, he explains. 'But authentic knowledge and information in the West is often diluted, perhaps because a teacher has not received the complete transmission or perhaps certain knowledge is lost in translation.'[15]

THERE IS A COMPELLING ARGUMENT that identifies the Ryukyu Islands in the East China Sea, the largest of which is Okinawa, as the link between early Chinese martial arts and their spread into Japan. As the smallest and least populated of Japan's principal islands, Okinawa punches well above its weight in having been the birthplace of the country's primary martial arts. It was here, as the majority of historians maintain, that these skills developed into the fighting techniques most widely followed today. If asked to name the first martial art that comes to mind, in the same breath as kung fu most people would reply 'karate'. This discipline can trace its popularity in Japan back roughly a century, though worldwide recognition was to come after the Second World War when it was picked up by U.S. troops stationed in Okinawa. The real boom started in the 1980s with the release of action films like *The Karate Kid*.

Initially known as *Toudi* or 'Chinese Hand', this practice became increasingly popular as *Karate*, signifying 'Empty Hand', a term that did not come into general use until the twentieth century. 'This "China-hand" martial arts system gradually came out of hiding in the late nineteenth century, after the samurai era was over,' notes historian Jonathan Clements. 'In 1879, the last king of the Ryukyu Islands abdicated at the order of the Tokyo government, moving to the mainland and accepting the commiseration prize of becoming a marquis in the Japanese honours system.'[16] This school originated in Okinawa for the simple reason that Okinawans, who were forbidden to bear arms, needed to find a way to defend themselves against the Japanese warlords who over the centuries repeatedly overran and occupied the island.

From the 1950s to the 1990s, the ascension of karate was astounding. In 1954, in fact, even few Japanese had any familiarity with the martial art and those that did associated it with an Okinawan import. 'Today, hundreds of millions of people all over the globe not only know something about karate but, by conservative estimates, some fifteen million practise the art,' explains martial arts historian Bruce A. Haines. 'In the long run, however, the karate purist would still find this disturbing. To be more precise and to explain this irritation with concrete examples, I find the following to be particularly out-of-step with the progenitors of karate and its associated art forms.' Haines singles out karate tournaments whose referees and sponsors allow and often encourage violence and mayhem, and instructors who award ranks and colour belts on the basis merely of hours spent, or who charge exorbitant fees and bicker over the appointment of officers to head karate associations. Asian martial arts, he says, are now highly commercialized and in need of some kind of purification. 'Hopefully, this will remain an isolated instance of this kind of mayhem and karate will continue to develop into the positive force that Gichin Funakoshi [the founder of Shotokan Karate] dreamed of so long ago in Okinawa and Japan.'[17] Gichin Funakoshi, an Okinawan master, introduced the discipline to the Japanese mainland in the early 1920s. The name Shotokan is Funakoshi's pen name, which translates as 'the House of Shoto'. It is regarded by practitioners as the hardest-hitting school of karate.

There are theories to suit every taste with regard to the historical starting point of karate. One of the more exotic hypotheses has it that this discipline was based on Mekata, an ancient Okinawan dance that displays certain elements of martial arts. There is also speculation that in the fourteenth century, a group of families from Fujian Province in southern China migrated to Ryukyu, bringing with them the practice of kenpo with its early form of karate movements. Kenpo and karate emphasize punches and kicks, as well as blocks and throws. However, unlike most forms of karate, kenpo brings into play other techniques, such as joint locks and grappling. In essence, kenpo is a blend of mainland Japanese and Okinawan martial arts and also contains influences from Chinese martial arts. Another theory places the origin of karate in the early seventeenth century, at the time of the Satsuma invasion of Ryukyu. It is also said that a century later, the Chinese martial artist Koshokun paid a visit to Okinawa, bringing with him a hands-on discipline known as kumiai-jutsu, which laid the groundwork for the development of karate.

Once again, the *when* lies deep within the domain of guesswork. The fifteenth or sixteenth century CE would appear to be the most likely period in which the arts of combat made their appearance on the islands. It was not just a case of import–export. In all probability, the Ryukyu people possessed their own native styles of fighting, taking into account the centuries of almost constant warfare between the islanders.

Historian Jonathan Clements explains that the Ryukyu Islands became a portal by which many elements of Chinese culture, including the martial arts, were preserved and introduced to the Japanese mainland. In the early sixteenth century, Ryukyuan martial arts diverged into combat techniques practised by the island aristocracy, or illegal underground peasant rituals designed to teach self-defence. 'The disarming of the Ryukyuan people was twofold, since the islands were invaded and occupied in 1609 by the Satsuma clan of Japan, which ran them for the next two hundred years as a vassal state,' writes Clements. 'The Satsuma clan also imposed a weapons ban on the locals, leading to the rise of a unified local unarmed fighting system by 1629, using elements of Chinese style and usually practised in secret to avoid the attention of the samurai overlords.'[18]

The samurai, meaning 'one who serves', were knights of medieval Japan. They were retainers of the name 'daimyo', feudal lords who, as leaders of powerful battle-hardened groups, controlled the provinces of Japan from the beginning of the Kamakura period in 1185 to the end of the Edo period in 1868. The names 'samurai' and 'martial arts' must be mentioned in the same breath. This aristocratic class skilled in the ways of combat arose during the wars of the twelfth century between the Taira and Minamoto clans and crystallized in the Tokugawa (or Edo) period. Samurai were privileged to wear two swords and at one time had the right to cut down any commoner who offended them. They cultivated the martial virtues of indifference to pain or death and loyalty to their overlords. This was in accordance with the cult of bushido, 'the way of the warrior', the code of honour and conduct of the Japanese nobility. Bushido in itself forms a key component of the samurai way of life and, as such, it sets out the basic tenets that martial arts practitioners are required to follow. This encompasses a code of behaviour to be adhered to by the follower, not unlike the European concept of chivalry. In fact, starting in seventeenth-century Japan, bushido began to become identified with Confucian ethics, which stress what might now be considered gentlemanly behaviour.

'Japan's samurai class started out as the servants and spare younger sons of the imperial court, packed off to the north of the country to busy themselves on border wars with the local aborigines, marchland politics and similar endeavours,' says Clements.

> However, by the medieval period these samurai had acquired and tamed the Kantō plain, the largest and most productive area of flat land in the entire mountainous archipelago. Once beholden to the imperial court, the samurai came to dominate it, ushering in several centuries in which the Japanese emperors were mere figureheads, controlled or fought over by warring clans.[19]

The samurai remained the dominant class in Japan over a long period. The top-echelon samurai, known as the Bonin, held strong views on who should or, more precisely, should not be ruling their country. In this respect they came to pose a serious social problem and were largely responsible for overthrowing the ruling Shogun military dynasty in 1867. They also took part in the 1877 rebellion in the Satsuma region, Japan's southernmost province, under the leadership of their master Takamori Saigō. Revered by many as the last true samurai, Saigō was killed in battle by Japanese troops during his campaign to depose the imperial government. Once the revolt had finally been quelled the class was abolished, but as statesmen, soldiers and businessmen, former samurai proved to be instrumental in building modern Japan.

The legacy of the samurai is intrinsically linked to their country's martial arts traditions. One can confidently affirm that 'samurai' and 'combat skills' are joined at the hip. A list known as the *Bugei Juhappan*, dating from the early seventeenth- to late nineteenth-century Edo period, details eighteen fighting arts attributable to samurai origin. Among others, these include kenjutsu, or the art of the sword, sojutsu, which is fighting with spears, and kyujutsu, with archery.

It may be stretching a point to classify 'water techniques' or 'rope tying' as genuine martial arts practices. The samurai were the first sect to truly excel in the use of weaponry, specifically the longbow, spear and sword, all of which made their way into the world of martial arts through this Japanese warrior class.

The iconic image of the samurai is that of an armour-clad soldier bearing a sword, two in fact, for these are the battlefield instruments that came to symbolize his exalted rank. A terrifying battlefield sight was the approach of a force of samurai mounted on their horses, each wearing a long *katana* sword and a shorter *wakizashi* blade strapped to his waist. In his hand was clasped the longbow, by far the deadliest weapon in the samurai's arsenal, since it could rain death on an enemy position from a range of more than 90 metres (300 ft). The bamboo longbow was the samurai's most cherished armament for nearly five hundred years. It was more than 2 metres (7 ft) in length and its user needed to be expert in firing arrows from horseback. When the longbow was put to use on the battlefield, an opposing force would often find their ranks decimated well before entering into close combat with the oncoming samurai furiously brandishing their swords.

Another tool of war, the *naginata*, was a lethal polearm consisting of a wooden shaft with a curved blade at the tip, while the *yari*, a long straight-headed spear, was used mostly for close combat. Samurai were skilled at deploying both these devices with deadly efficiency. The unique story behind the *naginata*, which measured up to 2.5 metres (8 ft) in length compared with some 6 metres (20 ft) for the *yari*, is that along with the long-handled bludgeon, it served as one of the weapons of choice for female Japanese warriors.

The caste of noblewomen known as *onna-bugeisha*, or 'female samurai', were trained in the art of conflict and the use of the straight-bladed *yari* as well as the curved *naginata* on the battlefield. Japan was beset by recurrent civil war throughout many centuries of its history. Women who became part of the fighting class usually did so because they were subjected to horrific brutality in these fratricidal conflicts. It therefore became a matter of survival for them to acquire battle skills and be able to wage war alongside their samurai menfolk.

These women stood out as a valiant reflection of their male counterparts. 'As such, they acted to consolidate and reinforce those qualities considered of fundamental importance to the emerging class of the *buke* [female class of warriors],' according to Oscar Ratti and Adele Westbrook in their narrative of samurai history. 'The product of a particular system, the samurai woman became its soundest basis and transmitter.'[20] There is one notable example of a woman who gives the lie to the popular perception of medieval Japan as an exclusively male domain. This is the twelfth-century warrior Hōjō Masako, known as Masa, the wife of the first Kamakura shogun, Minamoto Yoritomo. After his death, Masa ascended to the position of de facto ruler of Japan. Though not officially acknowledged as the empress, she nevertheless wielded great power and influence over the empire.

Women students practising jujitsu.

In the course of their Asian migration some 1,300 years ago, the martial arts made their journey across the Sea of Japan to the Korean Peninsula. Tradition has it, though this is strenuously disputed by some scholars, that at one point in the seventh century CE the Korean discipline that would become known as taekwon-do was introduced to this country by Won Kwang, the celebrated monk of Koryo, the ancient dynasty that gave its name to Korea. The name of this martial art signifies hand (*Tae*), foot (*Kwon*) and way (*Do*). In effect, the use of the unarmed practitioner's foremost attack tools.

Of the three reigning kingdoms of the Korean Peninsula at that time, Silla bore the distinction of being the only one with a queen on the throne: Sun-Duk, who achieved fame by importing Chinese martial arts into Korean society. 'She impressed the emperor [of China] by sending her best young warriors to the Emperor Kao-Tsu for training in the martial arts,' Peter Lewis writes. 'Song-Duk even drew up a special code of ethics to combine honesty, bravery, loyalty and justice with martial skills, so that her young warriors would be more than just fighting machines. This code was called Hwarang-Do, "the way of flowering manhood".'[21] Hwarang-Do, as it is practised today, is a modern development of an ancient Korean school of combat. It is steeped in mysticism, unsurprising given that the culture of Korea itself is entrenched in myth.

To appreciate this, look no further than the Sul Sa, a clandestine cult that formed part of this art in the 6th century CE. Its followers were believed to possess supernatural powers, acquired over years of gruelling physical and mental training. The Sul Sa were said to be endowed with spectacular athletic prowess, some bordering on the realm of sheer magic, such as their alleged ability to walk on water in special flat-bottom boots.

For the next five centuries taekwon-do training became compulsory for all men of Koryo. There can be no doubt that the name taekwon-do is synonymous with Korean martial arts. In its modern form, it is in essence the coming together of several Korean combat arts grouped under a homogeneous training format that came about in the mid-twentieth century. 'Originally, the system was used as a means of physical conditioning and hand-to-hand combat for Korean military personnel,' explains Michael Rosenbaum.[22] University students throughout Korea began taking up this new method of fighting. Taekwon-do training dojos began to appear throughout the country, and by the mid-1960s its popularity had spread to America.

Other schools have emerged in Korea over the centuries. Hapkido is a modern discipline as well as being a rather unusual one, in that it is not so much a fighting art as a method of self-defence. Its teachings centre on repelling an aggressor and only once that has been achieved, mainly through the use of joint locks, grappling and throwing, does the practitioner return a devastating selection of kicks and punches to put an adversary out of action. It should not be confused with the modern Japanese art of aikido, which places greater importance on spirituality and the pursuit of harmony and peaceful conflict resolution.

It is important to grasp the key principle underlying the classic martial arts, that violence should not be the objective of any serious student or seasoned practitioner. This truism has been emphasized by scholars and historians for centuries. In modern times, it has been espoused by writers and martial artists like Joe Hyams, who states unequivocally that the martial arts, in their finest form, are much more than a contest between two opponents, which itself is nothing more than a means of two people inflicting damage upon one another. 'Rather, for the true master, karate, kung-fu, aikido, wing-chun, and all the other martial arts are essentially avenues through which they can achieve spiritual serenity, mental tranquility, and the deepest self-confidence,' he says.[23]

Japanese kendo is the foremost example of how classic martial arts evolved from practical self-defence techniques into a discipline rich in philosophical and ideological meanings tied to spirituality and nationalism. Kendo practitioner and scholar Jiongyan Huang explains that if we were to take a closer look at Japanese martial arts practised today, we would find them often associated with words and phrases such as spirituality, personal development and self-cultivation.

> This is especially the case in kendo and iaido where kendo is the successor of early Japanese swordsmanship and iaido the sword-drawing art. Unlike unarmed budo like karate and judo, which have a noticeable aspect of being useful for physical self-defence, armed budo such as kendo and iaido are devoid

of such aspects and purely focus on spirituality and the training of mind.[24]

Jiongyan Huang points out that much like Krav Maga in Israel, a fighting art founded in the 1930s, kendo has undergone a significant ideological transformation, shifting its emphasis on spiritual and ethical values to intertwine with Japan's socio-political landscape, particularly during the Meiji period and the Second World War. Krav Maga was created with the aim of embracing techniques of other martial arts and combat sports to provide instruction for conscripted soldiers of the Israeli Defense Forces (IDF).

'While Krav Maga became a symbol of Israeli resilience and self-reliance, kendo came to embody Japan's values of loyalty, discipline and self-sacrifice during the war,' he says. 'Both martial arts, although culturally unique, illustrate how traditional combat systems can be re-contextualized as symbols of national strength, reflecting and shaping each country's identity and ideological goals.'[25]

Dojo aikido practice with swords.

As Japan moved into the militaristic climate of the 1930s, the government increasingly appropriated kendo as a means of fostering loyalty and a martial spirit in youth. By the early Shōwa period of the twentieth century, kendo had become a compulsory subject in schools and was adapted to emphasize combative techniques, aligning with Japan's preparation for war. Techniques and pedagogy were adjusted to promote aggressive and sacrificial fighting, with the shinai, a Japanese sword made of bamboo, shortened to encourage realistic, forceful strikes. This era of militarized kendo aimed to cultivate unwavering loyalty to the nation and readiness for combat, marking a

Krav Maga, a martial art designed for the Israeli military.

departure from its earlier, more recreational and competitive focus. The shift redefined kendo's concept of 'self-defence', elevating it from the personal level to a form of national defence.

The role of kendo in Japan has continuously oscillated between practicality and spirituality. Before the Tokugawa period of the seventeenth to mid-nineteenth century, swordsmanship served a practical function, essential for the samurai class in warfare and self-defence. However, in the peaceful Tokugawa era, this practical skill transformed into a more spiritualized form known as 'flowery swordsmanship', emphasizing kata practice and ritual over combat. After 1868, at the end of the Meiji period, swordsmanship was reinvented as kendo. It was employed as a tool for nation-building and reached its peak during the Second World War, where it became instrumental in instilling militaristic values and preparing individuals for battle. In the post-war era, militaristic ideologies were removed and kendo underwent a 'civilising' process, reintroduced as a democratic sport focused on peace, self-cultivation and personal growth.

2

WHENCE TO WHERE

Anyone with a casual interest in martial arts would almost certainly point to Japan as the homeland of the most celebrated of these fighting skills. This is understandable, for the list of conventional martial arts brought into vogue by channels such as contemporary literature and films of the Bruce Lee variety is extensive, and the martial arts are performed by many millions of enthusiasts in immersive teaching dojos across the globe. Aikido, judo, karate, jujitsu and kenpo are some of the most famous martial arts typically associated with Japan. It must be noted, however, as was brought to light in the previous chapter, that some of these schools had found their way into Japanese society via their Asian neighbour China.

Japan cannot today claim exclusivity as the training ground for the multitude of martial arts schools that have spread across the world. Consider the example of jujitsu, which some of the faithful assert can trace its roots back more than 3,000 years to India. While there is no historical evidence to support this claim, it is beyond doubt that no single country today, including Japan, can claim a monopoly on this fighting skill. In the early twentieth century, a new mixture of hand-to-hand combat made its appearance in Brazil, introduced by the Japanese entrepreneur and no-holds-barred prizefighter Mitsuyo

Maeda, who had emigrated to that country where he pioneered and promoted what was to become Brazilian jiujitsu.

In 1925 Maeda, who had Latinized his first name to Otávio, set up a jiujitsu academy in partnership with Carlos Gracie, the son of his Brazilian sponsor Gastao Gracie, a local politician. Another of Gracie's sons, Hélio, was a young man of slight physique and delicate health, who nonetheless was determined to participate in this exciting new activity. From observing his brothers in class, Hélio gradually devised a fighting system that was less punishing, one which he could follow even if his siblings considered it a watered-down version of their martial art. Hélio introduced new techniques, most importantly in leverage and timing, bringing them to a level that made him feel comfortable in his training sessions. Several years later, his efforts took shape as the contemporary school of Brazilian jiujitsu, practised today by an estimated 3 million people in that country.

Street violence has always been viewed as a feature of Brazil's urban life, especially in São Paulo and Rio de Janeiro. Carlos Gracie's eldest son, Carlson, in carrying on the family tradition, rose to become a Brazilian jiujitsu 9th degree red belt. He was aware that the vast majority of street fights end up on the pavement. With that in mind, he prioritized a system of grappling techniques that effectively bring an adversary to the ground and neutralize that person's ability to resist.

'The ideal takedown is when you are executing techniques that are high percentage, low risk and reasonably simple to pursue,' advises Rodney Stewart, an expert in aikido and the less widely known Russian martial art of Systema. 'Dynamic explosiveness, flexibility, speed and strength are all part of the equation but timing is the main principle.'[1]

This martial art can also be used to treat certain mental health concerns and psychological triggers. Alex Channon, a senior lecturer in physical education and sport studies at the University of Brighton, says that Brazilian jiujitsu can serve as a therapeutic tool for persons afflicted with personal trauma. Channon cites military veterans suffering from post-traumatic stress disorder (PTSD). 'In many cases, military service was the only life they knew,' he says. 'Leaving the forces can often cause mental trauma. I have found a programme of Brazilian jiujitsu to have a positive impact on their lives. A sixty-day programme delivered by the research gamekeeper REORG Charity has brought about a rapid improvement in PTSD symptoms.'[2]

With the passage of time, Brazilian jiujitsu developed its own style of combat, while also adopting a number of tenets that set it apart from the more mainstream schools practised in Japan, the United States and other countries. Self-defence took on a more prominent function in countering an attack from an armed opponent, a useful skill in Brazil's urban centres. Grappling also came to play a key role, while another principle, known as *Vale Tudo* (anything goes) stands out as full-contact techniques with few restraints on delivery. This fostered the development of what has become the most violent of all the fighting schools followed today, Mixed Martial Arts, or MMA.

Brazilian jiujitsu was the starting point of MMA, but what could in fairness be described as organized savagery has, in one form or another, been a spectator sport since Antiquity. Taking it back nearly three millennia to the Olympics in ancient Greece, there are records of combatants performing before spectators a mix of what we would recognize as boxing and wrestling, albeit with fewer restraints. This was branded Pankration, an unarmed sport that included kicking, joint locks and neck chokes on the ground, a forerunner to modern MMA. Taking bits and pieces from judo, karate and other disciplines,

MMA now attracts a vast number of adherents worldwide, with more than 2.5 million followers in the United States alone. MMA is in effect an amalgamation of techniques drawn from long-established schools of fighting, so why the enduring attraction of taekwon-do, kendo or any of the historical martial arts? The answer lies precisely in the appeal of their discipline, tradition and, not least of all, practitioners wanting to avoid becoming another statistic in the high rate of serious injuries that are sustained by MMA devotees.

MMA has excited the fighting spirit of millions around the globe, yet it might well be a mistake to think that this discipline has solved the problem of self-defence and that we should just replace traditional martial arts wholesale with MMA gyms. 'In MMA, while the pre-fight build-up is an attempt to replicate the bluster stage of a real fight, there is no possibility of de-escalation. The fighters are contractually obliged to fight each other for an extended period of time, far longer than any real fight would last,' martial arts historian John Tasker, a professor at Cardiff University, tells me.

> This is part of the appeal. The social aspects of 'real fighting' are removed or manipulated so that events move inevitably towards a violent and entertaining climax. But in the infinitely varied and variable 'real world', would it not be better for people to have an understanding of their own physiological and emotional responses, their habitual reactions to aggression and antagonism and an awareness that most confrontations do end in climbdown or stalemate if handled relatively calmly?[3]

Russia, like Brazil, does not immediately spring to mind as the likely birthplace of an indigenous martial art. But this should not come as a surprise, given the country's historical need to find ways to protect itself against aggressors. From the thirteenth century onward, Russia has suffered invasions by foreign powers, from the Mongolian hordes of Genghis Khan to Napoleon's Grand Armée, the Japanese incursion of 1905 and the Nazi offensive of the Second World War. The Russians have throughout the country's history been obliged to defend their territory against enemies deploying different styles of weaponry and combat, in battles fought in glacial winters and scorching summers, in terrain ranging from marshland to snow-capped mountains. Vastly outnumbered in many battlefield encounters, the Russian forces began to build a tactical system that could be deployed against an aggressor, whatever the circumstances. This fighting skill took the name of Russian martial arts. About 25 years ago, the name of the form taught by Vladimir Vasiliev and Mikhail Ryabko was changed to Systema. As the title implies, it is a system that roughly complies with the conventional parameters of a martial art, in that it teaches a set of tactics based on specific principles of instinct, strength and speed. Russian-born Vasiliev received his Systema training from Ryabko, who had worked in the Ministry of Interior Security Department as a trainer of the Minister's security guards. Vasiliev moved to Canada and in 1993 he founded Systema Headquarters, the first school of the martial art outside Russia.

Where Systema differs from karate or judo, for instance, is that it does not adhere to a strict set of rules or a rigid structure. Before it was exported to Europe and North America, Systema was the Russian gold standard of defensive fighting techniques. Joseph Stalin's bodyguards, suitably known as *Sokoli Stalina*, *sokoli* being the Russian term for 'falcons', were trained in the tactics of Systema. Operatives of the KGB, the Soviet-era spy network, were experts in this school of close combat, which on more than one occasion served them well on high-risk missions. 'The goal of Stalin's team, called The Falcons, was to have a system that combined all three levels of human abilities – the physical, the psychological and the psychic,' says martial arts expert Rodney Stewart. 'The secret was to develop tactics that would not look like martial actions and were so subtle that when they were applied it would be difficult to see what happened and how.'[4]

Systema instructor Matt Hill first took an interest in martial arts when he was twelve years old. He trained in karate for two years and then moved on to aikido, which he practised diligently until he was 24. His commitment to the Japanese martial art encouraged him to travel to Iwama in Japan, where he took up residence in the original dojo of aikido's founder Morihei Ueshiba under the tutelage of Morihiro Saito Sensei.

While training his way up to 5th Dan, Hill spent his days working on the land and cleaning the dojo and temple, while sleeping in the dojo at night. When not attending classes, a typical day consisted of cleaning duties, farming and serving his teacher, in exchange for which he received instruction in aikido. On his return to England, Hill joined the British Army and enrolled at Sandhurst Royal Military Academy, where he boxed and taught a few sessions in aikido, before being commissioned into the Parachute Regiment.

'At the end of my Army career, I came across Systema,' he says.

> I went to a seminar and met Mikhail Ryabko and Vladimir Vasiliev, Systema's founders. I was blown away at the seminar and realised that Systema is more about principle than technique. About six years later I went to Vladimir Vasiliev's summer camp north of Toronto and I have to say that it changed my life, along with my perspective of what constitutes a martial

art. The week I spent training in the forest was a physical and psychological healing process. About a year after the visit to Vladimir, I decided to go professional and devote my teaching exclusively to Systema.[5]

As Hill explains it, Systema is unlike other martial arts in that it is not based on technique. The discipline is broad and deep aimed at developing the physical, psychological and warrior spirit of the student. There are four principles that come together in training: breathing, natural movement, relaxation and posture. The art can be spontaneously creative and intuitive. There is an emphasis on improving and maintaining the student's health. All movements should feel natural, enabling the body to adapt to different situations.

'It is a psychologically healing activity,' says Hill 'in which you come to understand the nature of fear and learn to move with spontaneity and calm.' He says a good number of women are taking an interest in Systema to better manage anxiety and build self-confidence.

Curiously enough, the person whose profile soars above that of all public figures in Russia, namely athletic Vladimir Putin, has never shown an interest in his country's national martial art. However, he has made efforts to promote the indigenous school of sambo fighting by designating 16 November a day of national celebration in honour of it, which grew to prominence in the USSR in the 1930s. Sambo is an acronym for the Russian *Samo-oborona bez oruzhia*, which translates as 'self-defence without weapons'. It is a relatively obscure grappling art that comes into use in unarmed combat, using techniques similar to various styles of wrestling. Hence, to classify it as a genuine martial art is treading dubious waters.

Many of sambo's techniques can be found in other schools of fighting, with the addition of several Russian wrestling techniques, though supporters hotly deny any allegations that it is a plagiarism of judo, the classic Japanese martial art. They point to its ancient history, claiming an ancestry that can be traced back a thousand years to warfare between the Slavs and the Turkic Pecheneg tribes of Central Asia. There have been claims that its style is embedded in judo, citing few obvious differences between the two schools, though Russian fans vigorously refute any accusations of bootlegging. The Russian sportsman and academic Anatoly Arkadievich Kharlampiev, who started his career as a circus trapeze artist, is credited with being the pioneer and, from the 1940s onward, Russia's most ardent promoter of modern sambo. Under the guidance of this 'scholar-sportsman', sambo's techniques were refined and perfected. They spread into general use as a self-defence system and have become part of the training programmes of the Russian police, regular military and commando units. Following his death in 1979, a film was produced in memory of this outstanding personality, titled *The Invincible*. Tournaments known as A. A. Kharlampiev's Memorial are held every year in Moscow for the International Sambo Cup.

Putin has been a judo devotee for a good part of his life. He was awarded his 8th Dan black belt in 2012, at the age of sixty, the first person in his country to have reached this level in the Japanese martial art. A decade later, after Russia's invasion of Ukraine, Putin fell into disgrace in the martial arts community. The International Judo Federation declared that he was no longer entitled to hold a black belt and removed him as Honorary President of the organization. This decision was taken a few days after World Taekwondo (WT), the governing body of the Korean martial art, stripped Putin of his honorary 9th Dan black belt. Incidentally, Donald Trump retains an honorary 9th Dan black belt of his own, awarded to him in 2021 by the same South Korean organization.

Sambo at the 2015 European Games:
Andrei Kazusionak (BLR) vs Ashot Danielyan (ARM).

Sambo is undoubtedly one of the most brutal schools of combat claiming to merit a place among the martial arts. The rear-naked choke (RNC), considered a fundamental submission procedure in Brazilian jiujitsu and MMA, has on several occasions been taken to the limit in sambo, at times with fatal results. This is a technique designed to restrict blood flow to the brain, potentially rendering an opponent unconscious. Executed from behind, the attacker wraps one arm around the opponent's neck, positioning the crook of the elbow under the chin. The hand of that arm then reinforces the choke by gripping the opposite bicep or shoulder, while the other hand presses against the back of the opponent's head. By applying pressure from both sides, the choke compresses the carotid arteries, cutting off blood flow and forcing submission, usually causing loss of consciousness within seconds.

Where did the technique originate? 'In short, there is no definitive answer,' says John Tasker.

> The earliest apparent description of a rear-naked choke comes from the Greek traveller Pausanias around the second century CE. He describes how Arrhichion, a fighter in the Pankration games – a hybrid competition involving wrestling with strikes in ancient Greece – managed to win the match by dislocating his opponent's toe, despite being choked to death in the process. The description of the fatal choke matches exactly how we see the technique performed today.

Tasker says that despite there being an argument that the technique originated in ancient Greece, no one is seriously suggesting tracing a direct lineage from then to now.

> It is more likely that the technique was 'discovered' spontaneously in different grappling cultures at different times. In Brazil it is known as *mata leao* or 'lion killer', with an associated myth involving hunting tribes in the Amazon subduing lions and panthers with the move. In the U.S. and the UK, the move became popular in the pro wrestling circuit [and was] known as a 'sleeper hold'.[6]

The term 'rear-naked choke' is a translation of the Japanese term, used in judo. 'Rear' refers to the fact that the attacker must be behind their opponent, while 'naked' refers to the fact that it does not involve use of the *gi*, meaning 'traditional uniform'. This was the expression that came to be used by commentators for the Ultimate Fighting Championship (UFC), the American MMA promoter headquartered in Las Vegas, where the phrase and the move were popularized in the West. The first ever UFC fight was finished with a RNC and since then it has been by far the most effective method of submission, with around half of all victories achieved by its use.

The practices that came together to create MMA include one that is native to a country not readily associated with martial arts. China, Japan and, later, Korea are recognized as the progenitors of the schools that have attracted the greatest number of adherents worldwide: karate, judo, taekwon-do, aikido, to name a few of the most familiar disciplines. MMA is heavily influenced by Thai boxing, Muay Thai (formerly 'Siamese boxing' in English). The skill that came into being is known as the Science of Eight Limbs because it teaches the use of different striking parts of the body to make eight points of contact. The earliest chronicles place the origin of Muay Thai in the thirteenth century CE, coinciding with the establishment of the first kingdom of Siam, under the rule of King Ram Khamhaeng. Siam, the country that was renamed Thailand in 1939, in those early days was surrounded by hostile neighbours, which led to the development by the kingdom's army of defensive tactics with weapons and open-handed techniques.

Muay Thai is deemed to be one of the most challenging of all combat sports. There remains, however, a question mark over whether it conforms to the definition of a martial art. It is a remarkable fighting practice that has much in common with MMA and kickboxing and, for that very reason, there are those who do not accept it as a true martial art. 'Putting it under the banner of "martial art" serves for convenience rather than accuracy, since it has never been an art of war,' notes historian David Mitchell. 'It involves no practice of forms (patterns, or *katas* as they are known in karate) or basic techniques and no pretence to improving the character. It is quite simply a superb fighting art which, in its native form, is surely the most deadly of all.'[7] Taekwon-do instructor Keiron Henderson takes the opposite view. 'I would argue that Muay Thai is the complete martial art, but ruinous on the body,' he says.

> Muay Thai is a true martial art because it teaches a defined set of skills, which in combination are specific to the art. It springs from what the French would call a *terroir*. It is uniquely identifiable as Thai, with tradition, etiquette, ritual and ceremony that place the emphasis on competition between two individuals. There is modesty in victory and concern for the defeated. Braggadocio is not respected in Muay Thai. Annihilation of

Muay Thai in action.

the opponent is not the goal. The goal is the wholehearted, skilful practice of the art.[8]

Muay Thai has acquired extensive popularity around the world, especially among newer generations of enthusiasts. When software engineer Josiah Farrelly was sixteen years old, he found himself looking for ways to release what he describes as a lot of pent-up aggression. In 2016 he quite by chance came across Bloodline, a gym located near his home in the London Borough of Hackney, which offered classes in Muay Thai. Farrelly started attending classes four to five times a week. Work commitments have now forced him to reduce this to a couple of weekly classes, though he says he would like to increase the number of sessions.

'I was drawn in mostly by curiosity,' he says. 'The instructors were good professional fighters. I trained intensively in my first year and found it a way to improve mental and physical discipline to relieve exam stress. Muay Thai brought improvement to something that couldn't be achieved by school.'[9] After finishing school, he took his skills to the University of Bristol, where he trained a number of his fellow students.

'The influence of Muay Thai has impacted my life,' he says. 'I like the honesty of it. It's about self-confidence, how I carry myself, feeling comfortable in my body, as well as forming bonds of friendship. Nothing does this quite so well as being punched in the face. It builds camaraderie.'

Farrelly explains that there is no belt or grading system. 'You are as good as you are,' he says. 'Your ability to fight is reflected in your personal techniques. In my view it is more direct and efficient than other martial arts. You do not carry weapons. Your fists, feet and knees are some of the fighting tools available.' There have been some abortive attempts to introduce coloured *Prajiads* (ceremonial armbands) as a means of grading, but this is by no means common or widespread and any belt or grading system used in a gym is typically a red flag.

Competitions at the lower level, in the UK at least, may also be split into 'classes', from Interclub (also known as smokers, or N-Class) of C, B or A in terms of experience. Typically the lower classes have more restricted rulesets to better preserve the health of the fighters. For instance, elbows or knees to the head are not allowed. You're considered 'professional' when fighting in A-class or above (below that being amateur); this is typically the point where it's full ruleset: no padding aside from boxing gloves.

Somewhat less prominent in the public eye are the combat sports of Thailand's Southeast Asian neighbours Vietnam and Malaysia. Việt Võ Đạo, which translates as 'the way of Vietnamese martial arts', rather than stemming from a single discipline, developed as a fusion of individual techniques, some of which are practised with weapons. 'The last great master of the system was Nguyen Loc and in 1938 he collected all the separate elements and brought them together under one title.'[10] This was Việt Võ Đạo, or Vovinam, moulded on on established, eclectic Vietnamese techniques. Nguyen Loc's style of fighting was taken abroad by Vietnamese refugees who left their country during or after the twenty-year war between north and south Vietnam. The majority of these expatriates settled in France, their former colonial ruler. Vovinam's unarmed methods in many ways bear a resemblance to karate and taekwon-do, with the addition of some spectacular grappling techniques. The 'jumping scissors' is one example, in which an attacker leaps off the ground to tackle an opponent by wrapping his legs around the neck, shoulders or knees. This has got to be one of the trickiest unarmed procedures performed in any style of unarmed combat.

Thailand shares a border with Malaysia, the homeland of another martial art, known as Silat. It came about as a means of personal defence intended to protect the populace against the threat of invasion by neighbouring countries, primarily Thailand and, to a lesser extent, China, which controlled ports in Malaysia 2,500 years ago as a link to its trade with India. The feared physical invasions never took place, but the cultural influence of these two countries in Silat is evident.

Silat can be linked to karate, at least in spirit, as a 'people's' martial art in as much as it came about to protect ordinary citizens, in the way the Japanese school was practised during its foundational days in Okinawa. The purest manifestation of this Malaysian art can be appreciated in villages, rather than in urban schools. In rural areas, Silat demonstrations are often staged to enliven celebrations, where participants perform to the accompaniment of musicians. Let it not be assumed, however, that Silat is simply a ritual for adding merriment to village festivities and weddings: there exists a popular version of this art that involves the use of swords and knives in a deadly capacity.

Many miles from the lands that spawned the world's leading martial arts, sitting in the middle of the South China Sea, lies the Philippines. It was some five centuries ago on these islands that the natives developed a system of violent techniques to defend themselves against the Spanish colonists. It was called Escrima, a derivation of the Spanish *esgrima* (swordsmanship). The imperial invaders felt themselves under threat of violent attack from these machete- and dagger-wielding enemies, whose practice was strictly banned. Study and training in the art carried on in secret for nearly four hundred years, until the Spanish were ousted and replaced by the Americans in the Spanish–American War of 1898.

The country's new colonial masters took a more benign approach to their subjects. The relationship was as easy-going as could be expected between foreign conquerors and those under their rule, to the point that the U.S. Army allowed Escrima practitioners to carry machetes, which they used with fearsome efficiency in guerrilla operations against the Japanese, who invaded the country in 1941.

An Escrima match is an exhilarating spectator event, in which opponents swing batons instead of bladed weapons, clashing with almost every move and clubbing an opponent who fails to dodge or repel an oncoming blow. Escrima is now officially recognized as the Philippines' national martial art and can boast a large number of celebrated practitioners worldwide, including Bruce Lee, who took this style of fighting to the screen in two of his most famed action films, *Enter the Dragon* (1973) and *Game of Death* (1978).

MORE THAN SIX MILLION PEOPLE in the United States actively participate in martial arts, more than in any other Western country, according to Statista, the online platform for data and business intelligence. Brazilian jiujitsu, karate, taekwon-do and MMA take the lead in terms of total participants.[11] But by sheer force of numbers, China is at the forefront of practitioners. While nobody knows with precision how many Chinese might take part in one or more of these disciplines, it is generally believed that the figure could easily run into the tens of millions.

The mid-twentieth century brought a seismic shift in the centre of gravity for martial arts. The spotlight moved from Japan to Korea. Taekwon-do, commonly and not without some justification called Korean karate, given the similarities of many of its techniques, formally acquired its own name in 1955. What is known about taekwon-do's beginnings, apart from the legendary tale of its introduction by a Buddhist monk in the seventh century CE, is that one or another form of unarmed combat had been in use in the Korean Peninsula for more than 2,000 years. The nobles and knights of ancient Korea developed a fighting technique using their hands and feet. These warriors were known as *Hwa Rang Do*, the name adopted by a school of semi-full contact fighting in its own right, which began to flower in the 1960s. From its earliest days, the art of taekwon-do has been passed on from generation to generation without any fundamental changes in technique. This martial art has since its formal debut in the West experienced a spectacular growth in popularity. It is now recognized as the most widely practised martial art in the world, with an estimated 50 million devotees in more than 120 countries.

Mental and physical discipline are the underlying mainstays of taekwon-do, as defined in the five tenets students are expected to embrace: courtesy, integrity, perseverance, self-control and indomitable spirit. 'The physical manifestations in the form of lethal attacks and the breaking of objects are much like the visible part of an iceberg,' explains Grandmaster Duk Sung Son. 'They are only part of the whole and, although they are the most dramatic, they are not the most important. These physical displays are, of course, important, but not as ends in themselves. They simply provide a measure of progress in tangible physical terms, a datum.'[12]

As well as being the most popular of the martial arts, taekwon-do also holds the title of being the most controversial discipline since its establishment in Korea more than seventy years ago. Some Korean historians claim that karate was an offshoot of taekwon-do, when in fact the opposite is a far more plausible version. It should not be forgotten that Japan was an occupying force in Korea during the

Second World War. During that time the influence of Japanese martial arts took hold in the country. This was especially true of karate, taught to Koreans who chose to fight alongside their Japanese overlords.

Taekwon-do, as it is practised today, must be mentioned in the same breath as its founder. General Choi Hong Hi, a North Korean by birth, acquired his first contact with martial arts as a student of karate. Choi was a pivotal figure in the development of this inherently Korean martial art. The founder of taekwon-do's representative body, the International Taekwon-Do Federation (ITF), in 1966, Choi is revered by his followers as the true founder of the martial art. The ITF soon gained associations in nine countries, from Vietnam to the United States, where it was taught at West Point Military Academy.

As a young martial arts aspirant, Choi went to Japan to train in karate. He returned to Korea in 1942, where he went into hiding to avoid being forced to fight alongside the Japanese occupation forces. He was soon arrested and condemned to death for treason but was fortunate enough to escape execution only three days after Korea's liberation. Choi was commissioned by the South Korean Army, which he had helped to establish, and by 1954 he had been promoted to Brigadier General. The previous year, Choi had founded an academy in which he instructed men under his army command in the art of unarmed combat. After spending more than a decade building up the popularity of his school, Choi was appointed president of the Korean Taekwondo Association.

However, his professional life was soon marked by controversy. In 1962 Choi was forced to retire from the military due to his lack of support for President Park Chung Hee, who took power following a bloodless coup the previous year. As Choi became more vocally opposed to President Park, he came under harassment from the president for having introduced taekwon-do to North Korea. In 1972 he went into self-imposed exile in Canada, where he also located the ITF headquarters. Choi's enemies in the rival organization World Taekwondo (WT) denounce him as a dishonourable figure owing to what they allege was his 'defection' to North Korea; his supporters hail him as the leading light in the global spread of his martial art.

From the early 1970s, Choi had to endure a barrage of death threats from the Korean intelligence services, as well as several attempts to murder him. His son and daughter, who remained in Korea, were briefly kidnapped and threatened with execution if Choi refused to return from exile. His celebrated response was that he chose taekwon-do over his family members, who were subsequently released. Choi died of cancer in 2002 in Pyongyang, North Korea, where he is buried.

His students remember him as an inspiring teacher who expected his pupils to strive for perfection. 'I spent about fifteen years under the training of General Choi Hong Hi,' says Grandmaster Donato Nardizzi. 'The experience of studying directly from taekwon-do's founder provided me with essential knowledge about the art's philosophical as well as its technical aspects and historical development. Through his dedication to taekwon-do I learned the practice and teaching methods I use in my own classes.'[13]

Championed by the South Korean government, WT eclipsed its rival ITF in 1988 when it was entered as an Olympic sport at the 1988 Seoul Games. This was a purely political initiative, since both schools exhibit more similarities than differences of style. ITF and WT are famed for their spectacular high kicks, which are the most diverse of any martial art. In their sparring tactics, ITF uses a number of pre-arranged attacks, essentially a more rigid procedure of combat than WT's semi-free style. These distinctions vanish, however, once the instructor gives the signal to begin free sparring.

There is a third organization of significant size that merits a mention. It is known as ATA Martial Arts, the successor to the American Taekwondo Association (ATA). This association is indigenous to the United States, having been set up in 1969 in Nebraska by South Korean Grandmaster Haeng Ung Lee and his American co-founder partner Richard Reed. The ATA, now headquartered in Arkansas, takes third place among the major taekwon-do associations, with some 300,000 active members worldwide, nearly half of them training in the United States.

Lee advanced at breakneck speed in his taekwon-do career. In 1954 he earned his 1st Dan black belt in the space of one year, an almost unheard-of feat. After a stint in the Korean Army, training special forces, Lee came into contact with the American martial arts practitioner Reed, who sponsored Lee's move to the United States and with whom he became co-creator of ATA. In 1990 the ATA Master's Council conferred on Lee his 9th Dan, making him the world's youngest grandmaster. Ten years later and in keeping with time-honoured taekwon-do tradition, Lee was posthumously promoted to 10th Dan and awarded the title 'Eternal Grandmaster'. On Lee's death in 2000, U.S. President Bill Clinton's condolences were read to a crowd of 3,000 mourners in attendance at the grandmaster's funeral in Little Rock, Arkansas. As a token of remembrance, Lee's family members in the United States gifted an 8-ton traditional gate to the city, where ATA was headquartered, as a public memorial to Lee.

In attempting to define the disparities between the three major schools of taekwon-do, apart from the differences in patterns practised in each, it can be said that ITF is less restrictive in its sparring rules. Kicks and punches can be delivered to the head, as well as any front or side part of the body, including the face. Knees and elbows, headbutts and sweeps are not permitted, although some of these are taught in the training patterns. No strikes are allowed below the belt or to the back and competitors are penalized for turning their back to avoid a strike.

By contrast, WT has similar rules but does not allow hand strikes to the head or face. Target areas are limited roughly to the chest and abdomen, bringing it closer in line with the organization's sport-orientated code of ethics. Both federations reward jumping and spinning techniques with higher point scores. ATA, on the other hand, is in essence a blend of the two primary international schools and concentrates more on procedural skills in the dojang than combat in the ring.

Those who make taekwon-do or, for that matter, any of the traditional martial arts a primary factor in their lives will almost invariably emphasize the psychological and spiritual benefits to be derived from their chosen discipline. 'It's all about commitment,' says Daniel Beard, a London-based taekwon-do practitioner and instructor. 'So long as you don't give up, with time, training and a good instructor, you will always progress and improve your skills – even if you don't think yourself capable of it,' he said in an interview. Beard, a 26-year-old 4th Dan, began to take an interest in martial arts at the age of ten. His first formal contact was with kung-fu, which was his father's speciality. But after attending a local club for a couple of months, and not taking to it, he withdrew soon after. He visited a karate class but was not fully won over by this practice, which he found too rigid and lacking flexibility in its movements. Eventually, he settled on a third martial art, from which he never looked back.

'I decided to take up taekwon-do, which had a great deal of appeal for someone of my age,' he says. This initial encounter eventually took him body and soul into the world of the Korean martial art. 'The impact it has had on my life has been incalculable,' he says. 'What began as a hobby has become a full-time occupation for me. It is hard to measure how life would have been without it.'[14] Beard says it became the crucial element in his discipline and development as a person.

He had left university with a degree in computer science at a difficult time to be looking for work and found himself facing the question of what to do with his life. 'I decided to devote that extra time to taekwon-do,' he says. 'It turned out to be the best decision I've ever taken. It has brought me deep satisfaction and gave me a secure central point. Eventually after a year of being unable to find a job in software, I decided; I'm devoting so much of my time to taekwon-do already – why don't I make *this* what I do?'

When Beard first began training, he never thought he would reach black belt level.

> When I first reached red belt, I thought, *This is it for me. There's no way I'll ever be good enough to reach black belt.* Then, after training at red belt for a couple of years, my instructor came to me and told me I should go for a grading. After one failed attempt, I passed. When that happened, again I thought, *Well, this is it. There no way I'll ever be good enough for 2nd Dan*. Lo and behold, four years later my instructor tells me that not only am I ready but I'm overdue. I passed with flying colours that time. After that, I learnt to stop telling myself that I'm not good enough. I might not be now, but with consistent training and a little patience, I will be.

One of the chief benefits of regular practice has been learning to totally ignore provocative situations in the street or elsewhere. 'I feel completely comfortable walking the streets of London at night,' he says. 'I know that the first priority must be to get away from a potentially violent situation and not to be fearful.' This is a principle shared by most martial artists. Beard's ambition is to reach 7th Dan Master level. 'If you had told me six or seven years ago that I would have this in my sights, I would have thought you were mad,' he says. 'I am now completely confident I will achieve that goal – eventually, with a couple of decades of work.'[15]

IT WILL PERHAPS COME AS NO SURPRISE that the most idiosyncratic of the world's martial arts was conceived in Britain. In 1900 the English entrepreneur Edward William Barton-Wright opened the Bartitsu School in central London. Barton-Wright was a man of strong Asian connections, having been born in India and lived for a number of years in Japan. He was, at least in appearance, a typical upper-class Englishman of the early twentieth century, sporting a bushy moustache and flowery silk cravat.

During his sojourn in Tokyo, he developed a fascination with jujitsu, to the extent that he took with him to London two Japanese experts in the art, who were to instruct in the academy he planned to set up. Barton-Wright then took it upon himself to create a wholly new discipline, which he baptised Bartitsu, an eponym of his own surname. It was a close copy of the jujitsu he had followed in Japan, but its founder brought in elements of other practices, such as boxing, wrestling, French-style kickboxing and even fighting techniques that make use of the walking sticks carried by proper gentlemen of his day. Given its multiplicity of fighting ingredients, Bartitsu could be regarded as an early version of MMA. According to Paul Bowman, in his book *The Invention of Martial Arts*,

> The pioneering research carried out by scholars such as Emelyne Godfrey, along with the Bartitsu Society (which is orientated towards the historical reconstruction or reinvention of Bartitsu), has revealed that there were numerous and frequent news stories printed in the London press about Bartitsu and other forms of self-defence in the late Victorian and Edwardian eras of the 1890s and 1900s. It was most likely the news stories of this 'gentlemanly art of self-defence' that brought it into the consciousness of Sir Arthur Conan Doyle, who used it in the 1903 reprise of Sherlock Holmes, 'The Adventure of the Empty House'.[16]

In the short story 'The Empty House', originally published in *Colliers* magazine in 1903, Dr Watson passes out from shock when an elderly, deformed man who had been following him in the street turns up at his house and reveals himself to be Sherlock Holmes. Watson thought Holmes had fallen to his death, along with the notorious Professor Moriarty, in a cliff-top struggle between the two arch-enemies. 'We tottered together upon the brink of the fall,' Holmes explains.

> I have some knowledge, however, of baritsu [Conan Doyle's misspelling of Bartitsu], or the Japanese system of wrestling, which more than once has been very useful to me. I slipped through his grip and he with a horrible scream kicked madly for a few seconds and clawed the air with both his hands ... With my face over the brink I saw him fall for a long

way. Then he struck a rock, bounded off, and splashed into the water.[17]

It has been suggested that this was the key literary mention most likely to have helped rescue Bartitsu from being lost or forgotten to history. The Victorian and Edwardian interest in the martial art was certainly piqued by Conan Doyle's reference to it, especially among self-defence researchers looking at its history in Britain.[18]

There is no denying that many of Barton-Wright's techniques are as relevant to people now walking the streets of great urban centres as was the case more than a century ago. Knife attacks in cities like London make headlines on an almost daily basis. While martial arts instructors insist the most effective defence is to put some distance as quickly as possible between the attacker and the intended victim, it is not always possible to escape an assailant. In 1899 Barton-Wright published an article in a London magazine explaining how to deal with a knife attack: 'We will suppose that you have to pass through a locality late at night where there is likelihood of such an attack, and you do not want to run the risk of bringing yourself within the law by relying upon a revolver,' he wrote in *Pearson's Magazine*.

> Carry your overcoat upon your shoulders without passing your arms through the sleeves, in the style of a military cloak, with your right hand ready upon your left shoulder to use your coat in the way explained below, should the necessity arise. Be careful always to walk in the middle of the road. Directly your assailant attacks you, face him and wait until he is within a distance of two or three yards. Then envelop his head and arms by throwing your coat at him, with a sweeping, circular motion of the arm. This will obscure his view momentarily, but not

> your own, and will give you plenty of time to deliver your attack, which should take the form of a right-handed knock-out blow in the pit of the stomach.[19]

Popular literature abounds with martial-artist characters, heroic as well as villainous. Conan Doyle gave his readers a gallant one in the person of Sherlock Holmes, a practitioner of Bartitsu. The more infamous type is embodied in Ian Fleming's *Goldfinger*, the 1959 espionage novel in which the British agent 007, James Bond, hunts down the gold smuggler Auric Goldfinger, a suspected Soviet apparatchik. Goldfinger's Korean henchman Oddjob, whose real name is never revealed, is a formidable karate prodigy, whose skills are displayed in several episodes. To Bond's astonishment, the Korean lifts his hand high above his head and brings it down like an axe, splintering a heavy polished stair rail. Oddjob then takes off his hat and coat and in one long crouching stride with knees bent, he whirls off the ground.

> In mid-air his feet slapped together like a ballet dancer's, but higher than a ballet dancer's have ever reached. Then the body bent sideways and downwards and right foot shot out like a piston. There came a crashing thud. Gracefully the body settled back down on the hands, now splayed on the floor, the elbows bent to take the weight and then straightened sharply to throw the man back and up on his feet.[20]

A spectacular albeit questionable depiction of actual karate techniques.

Fleming himself displays a rather slapdash knowledge of karate, which he describes as 'a branch of judo', when he has Goldfinger explain to Bond that only three men in the world have achieved a black belt degree. The actual number is unknown, but it can safely be reckoned in the tens of thousands.

A far more intriguing martial arts figure in fictional literature than Oddjob is American billionaire Bruce Wayne, aka Batman. The 2008 film *The Dark Knight*, directed by Christopher Nolan, ranks as the abiding tale of Batman's war on crime in Gotham City. In the film the Caped Crusader corners the mob but is confronted with a new class of criminal on the rise, the Joker, a demonic character who drives Batman to the edge of insanity. Leaving that personal conflict aside, there is Batman's relationship with martial arts, which appears in the first page of the film's novelization. Batman uses kicking techniques to shatter the window of a speeding railway carriage in which lurks a foe intent on murdering Gotham's hero. 'A shadow on the floor alerted him that he was being attacked from behind and, without taking time to turn, he drove his elbow backward.'[21] An established martial arts move for putting an unseen attacker out of action.

Bruce Wayne spent time training at a monastery, where he practised meditation under the guidance of his master Ra's al Ghul. According to the novel, on Bruce's return to Gotham, his butler Alfred Pennyworth finds his master 'in an empty area, performing one of the strange, dancelike routines called a *kata* and whose purpose was to train in Asian martial arts'.[22] He explains that he had acquired his skills in the seven years he spent as a martial arts disciple in Korea.

The list of works of fiction with martial arts as the central theme would in itself fill a chapter. Children's author and Japanese Taijutsu black belt Chris Bradford has given his young fans a ten-book *Young Samurai* series, from *The Way of the Warrior* (2008) to *The Way of the Dragon* (2009) and *The Ring of Sky* (2012). Adult readers have turned Eric Van Lustbader's *The Ninja* (1980) and James Clavell's *Shōgun*

(1975) into bestsellers, to say nothing of Robert Twigger's *Angry White Pyjamas*, published in 1997, a *Sunday Times* runaway success and a Waterstones Book of the Year. Martial arts in literature is a phenomenon that has built up a huge number of devotees across the world.

3

HANDS OFF!

The fairer sex. The weaker sex. Damsels in distress! Terms of endearment braised in sarcasm, platitudes that effectively relegate women to the lower rank of the human species. This is not just laddish banter. It is not unknown for verbal misogyny to degenerate into physical abuse. In Britain alone, with its hypothetical culture of gender respect, violent attacks against women and girls have soared by nearly 40 per cent in recent times, to the extent that every year more than one hundred women are killed by men. In the United States, more than a third of women have suffered rape, physical violence or stalking by an intimate partner. These are established and widely known facts. Less extensively reported are the steps a growing number of women of all ages are taking to defend themselves and, if necessary, fight back through the medium of martial arts.

The history of women warriors who wielded fighting skills on a par with their menfolk stretches back many centuries and arises from all corners of the world. The samurai women have already been cited in this narrative. In Japan, the cradle of many of the classic martial arts, as well as in Korea, early chronicles speak of valiant women on the battlefield leading armies against enemy strongholds. Tomoe Gozen, who lived and fought in the twelfth century, rose to the rank of general and in 1182 CE she led three hundred samurai warriors to victory against 2,000 troops of the rival Taira clan.

These samurai women upheld their commitment to the caste's code of honour with the same fierce determination as their fellow male combatants. A woman samurai would without hesitation use her *kaiken*, a short-bladed dagger, to commit ceremonial suicide by cutting her throat if she found herself in danger of being captured by enemy forces or felt she had failed in her duty. Japan's samurai women were expertly trained in fighting and stood out as precursors of an ethos that in time to come would see a multitude of women taking part in the country's martial arts.

Moving forward to the modern era and with the focus on Japan, the life of nineteenth-century Yonamine Chiru attests to Okinawa's enduring martial arts heritage. Yonamine no Bushi Tsuru ('Yonamine the crane warrior'), as she was nicknamed, was the wife of Matsumura Sōkon, one of the island's most celebrated karate practitioners. She rose to the status of master by virtue of the martial arts background of her family. Yonamine Chiru's slender figure and beauty concealed an extraordinary aptitude for weightlifting and sumo wrestling. It was these skills that ultimately drew Sōkon to his future wife, with whom he would spend hours in sparring matches. After one exchange, Chiru congratulated Sōkon for the progress he had made against her. 'You have learned a valuable lesson, my husband, that in combat you should not distinguish between the sexes,' she said. 'An opponent is an opponent. Sometimes, as you may have learned, a woman can be much more dangerous than a man for that very reason.'[1]

Some men would have to learn this fact of life the hard way. Okinawans tell of how one evening, when Yonamine was walking home from a social gathering, three men emerged from the darkness of the surrounding woods. They looked at her maliciously, like predators ready to pounce on their supposed defenceless prey. 'Get out of my way or I'll have to punish all three of you!' Yonamine shouted. They laughed off her threats and positioned themselves to attack. She had learned from her father's teachings that in a confrontation with several assailants, one must move in such a way that the leader always remains between the defender and the others. Without further warning, she jumped on the man nearest her, knocking him to the ground. 'He blinked with a look of fear in his eyes as he saw how the placid and feminine face of that woman had transformed in an instant into a war mask.' She then delivered a kick to the temple of another assailant and a hammer blow to the third man's throat. Several hours later, Matsumura was returning home from the party along the same route. He was surprised to hear wailing noises coming from the bushes, where he discovered three men tied up like cattle.[2]

THE GENESIS OF WOMEN COMBATANTS stretches back some 1,700 years before the appearance of the samurais and over 9,500 kilometres (6,000 mi.) to the west of Japan. The fifth-century BCE Greek historian Herodotus wrote of the Amazons, an ancient class of warlike Mediterranean women whom he defined as physically equivalent to males and even as slayers of men. To the Greeks, the Amazons had been a real people, their existence never in doubt. The Greeks were not the only ones in Antiquity to accept the presence in their society of a superior breed of martial women. In nearby Italy the Etruscans erected bronze statues depicting wrestling matches between men and women. During the reign of the Achaemenid king Darius I, who ruled Persia in the sixth century BCE, a woman named Artunis, the daughter of one of Cyrus the Great's generals, was held in high esteem by fellow officers who regarded her as a formidable soldier. Anonymous women's graves, many of them roughly of that same period, have been unearthed to reveal a cache of battlefield weapons. In Egypt, women's sepulchres dating to the Pharaonic era have been found to contain an assortment of various military weapons. Archaeological digs in India and China have likewise uncovered evidence of an early female warrior class in their respective societies.

In fifth-century BCE China, the woman warrior Yuenü, popularly known as the Lady of Yue, rose to fame as an unparalleled master of the sword during the reign of King Goujian. Many Chinese still revere Yuenü as a major influence on swordsmanship, including Taijijian and other bladed-weapon practices used ceremoniously in tai chi. Plenty of folk tales are associated with the life of this extraordinary woman. Combining the study of philosophy with sword techniques learnt from her father, Yuenü inspired numerous popular fables. It was alleged that she had defeated 3,000 swordsmen to win a seven-day tournament that was regularly organized under China's Zhou dynasty. When the monarch asked about her remarkable methods, Yuenü was said to have replied, 'When fencing, though highly alert, the appearance is as calm as a fair lady's, but when in action, a vicious tiger emerges. Weak and exposed in appearance, but powerful when unleashed.'[3]

Another legendary Chinese martial artist, though one born far more recently, was the Buddhist nun Ng Mui, whose followers maintain that this remarkable woman, active during the early eighteenth century, was the founder of Wing Chun, a form of kung fu, the fighting art catapulted to worldwide cinema fame by Bruce Lee. Wing Chun is a relatively recent version of kung fu, having emerged from the Shaolin Temple of Southern China around three hundred years ago. As folklore has it, while residing in the temple Ng Mui took it upon herself to create a fighting method suitable for women. Her work earned the unofficial title of one of the leading martial artists, male or female, in China in the early 1700s. The tale relates that Ng Mui developed her techniques while observing a stork beating its wings to defend itself against a predator rodent.

Western culture has also produced women who aspired and succeeded in making a name for themselves in male-dominated combat arts. At roughly the same time that Ng Mui was perfecting the movements of Wing Chun, Londoner Elizabeth Wilkinson was engaging in bareknuckle prize fights in London's East End arenas. Wilkinson, who became Wilkinson Stokes after marrying her promoter and fellow boxer James Stokes, had also trained in several of the classic martial arts but her true passion was slugging it out in the ring.

Wilkinson's career took off in June 1722 after a famous bout with her long-standing foe Hannah Hyfield. In June of that year Wilkinson posted a challenge to her adversary in the London Journal: 'I, Elizabeth Wilkinson, of Clerkenwell, having had some words with Hannah Hyfield and requiring satisfaction, do invite her to meet me on the stage and box me for three guineas, each woman holding half-a-crown in each hand and the first woman that drops the money to lose the battle.' To which Hyfield promptly replied in the same journal: 'I, Hannah Hyfield, of Newgate Market, hearing of the resoluteness of Elizabeth Wilkinson, will not fail, God willing, to give her more blows than words – desiring home blows, and from her no favour: she may expect a good thumping.'[4] Elizabeth was declared the winner in a 22-minute match, after which her notoriety soared and she soon became the most famous woman boxer in Britain, earning her the nickname Lady Bareknuckles, the Boxing Champion of Clerkenwell.

The role of British women in martial arts moved into the limelight during the Suffragette movement of the early twentieth century. By 1905 violence had become a familiar feature of street protests by women demanding the right to vote. Groups of angry demonstrators would set alight public facilities such as postboxes, bricks were thrown at windows and, as a harbinger of tactics employed by today's Just Stop Oil activists, artworks in museums came under attack, while campaigners would routinely handcuff themselves to street railings.

There were those who took a different and decidedly effective approach to advancing their cause. Eminent among these was the diminutive 1.5 metres (4 ft 11 in.) Edith Garrud, who would go on to become the pioneer of instructing British women in the art of jujitsu. It was the logical discipline for Garrud, since its stress on body leverage instead of kicking or punching techniques was ideally suited to a person of her size. More than one gnarly London policeman was to

Edith Garrud, a British martial artist, suffragist and playwright, depicted in a 1910 *Punch* cartoon holding a jujitsu position.

find himself flat on his back while attempting to dislodge Garrud from a street demonstration.

Garrud studied jujitsu in London under the Japanese wrestler Sadakazu Uyenishi. She trained in her dojo alongside Emily Diana Watts, one of Europe's first female instructors, whose students included Mary Russell, Duchess of Bedford, an adventurous person in her own right who became known as the 'Flying Duchess' after qualifying as a pilot at the age of sixty. Garrud went on to impart her skills to the bodyguards who protected members of the militant suffragette organization the Women's Social and Political Union (WSPU). The media branded members of this group the Amazons, presumably unaware of the roots of the name conceived by Herodotus. Their prime responsibility was to protect WSPU orchestrator and guiding spirit of the suffragettes, Emmeline Pankhurst. If necessary, they were prepared to use their jujitsu, as well as the wooden clubs that they kept hidden under their frocks.

Garrud's street confrontations with the police were the stuff of legends. By 1909 she was giving demonstrations on how women can defend themselves against police aggression and 'establish the superiority of the trained feminist mind over untutored masculine strength'.[5] The *Evening Telegraph* ran a story the following year about Garrud's demonstration in a gym with a London bobby, who towered over her and believed he could subdue the suffragette without much effort.

> The pair tussled for a few minutes before Edith fell flat on her back allowing the policeman to tower over her. Just when he thought he had the advantage, she pushed her feet into his diaphragm and flung him over her head, causing him to somersault in mid-air and land with a thud on his back. When the

officer got up, he thoughtfully scratched his head and stated, 'If that had happened on the pavement instead of this mat, the police force would be one man short.'[6]

Garrud, playwright as well as martial artist, was a multitalented person who inspired biographers and filmmakers. As early as 1907, Garrud was featured as the protagonist in a documentary, *Jiujitsu Downs the Footpads*, which was produced by the film company Pathé. Four years later she choreographed the fight scenes for a play entitled *What Every Woman Ought to Know*. Her figure has continued to inspire filmmakers to this day. The 2015 film *Suffragette* (dir. Sarah Gavron) is a historical drama in which one character, Edith Ellyn, is based on Garrud's life. Ellyn, portrayed by Helena Bonham Carter, was originally named Caroline, but the actress changed it to Edith to honour Garrud's leadership in the struggle for women's rights. Garrud saw her combative work rewarded in 1928, when British women were given the vote on the same terms as men, albeit nearly a decade after U.S. Congress passed a law granting women equal voting rights.

In the decades that followed, American women discovered in Garrud and other resolute suffragettes a stimulus to take up the arts of self-defence. The militants of the 1920s protest movement had mainly embraced jujitsu in its different formats. The most prominent figure and most eminent judo celebrity in those post-suffragette years was June Tegner, pioneering martial artist and celebrity instructor. Throughout the 1940s and '50s, Tegner was a well-known face in newspapers and magazines. She was the matriarch of a dynasty of judo practitioners, which included her husband Jon, son Bruce and daughter Carol. She was a much sought-after Hollywood trainer, and one of the most celebrated images of her career shows film star

Humphrey Bogart lying flat on his back after being flipped over Tegner's shoulder. She had been training Bogart for his role in the 1949 film *Tokyo Joe*.

In terms of tenacity and groundbreaking achievement, the crown must go to the contemporary U.S. martial artist Cynthia Rothrock, who in fact holds the title of Queen of Martial Arts, an award granted by the California-based Martial Arts History Museum. Rothrock can lay claim to being the only woman in the country and indeed worldwide to have obtained black belt rank in no fewer than seven schools of martial arts.

'Through the martial arts, Rothrock became the hottest female action star in Asia and Europe,' says martial arts historian John Corcoran. 'She did it the hard way, first by becoming the queen of American forms competition, then the darling of the Asian film market.'[7] Rothrock, born in 1957, held the title of undefeated women's forms championship in number one position for four years.

As a young girl from Scranton, Pennsylvania, Rothrock took up karate at the age of thirteen and was awarded her black belt in a near record three years. Her interests later shifted to kung fu. By the time she was 28, Rothrock had already triumphed in five international forms and weapons championships, competing against men as well as other women. Then in 1985 she made her debut as an actress in the Hong Kong action film *Yes, Madam*. She co-starred in this film with Malaysian actress Michelle Yeoh, in the role of a police inspector in pursuit of stolen microfilm containing details of criminal gangs. 'I think we both just wanted to make this big, tough, kickass film that showcases women,' Rothrock said in a newspaper interview. In fact, the duo went so hard that the film's director had to cut one scene because both women were visibly injured. 'We were so bruised that every time we would fight, we would flinch,' Rothrock said.[8] Yeoh herself, from her unconventional take on a Bond girl in *Tomorrow Never Dies* (1997) to her high-flying kicks in the Ang Lee-directed film *Crouching Tiger, Hidden Dragon* (2000), has had a multi-decade career that defies stereotypes. In the Academy Award-winning 2022 film *Everything Everywhere All at Once*, Yeoh plays the superhero: a Chinese American immigrant mother who is called upon to save the world – and herself – by hopping across multiverses.

By 1988 Rothrock had established herself in the American action film world and has played lead roles in a number of movies. She also featured in the 1989 TV documentary *Women of the 21st Century*, which focused on women in sports and self-defence. 'I don't think it's strange that a girl from a small town like Scranton would wind up making a film with [Sylvester] Stallone [*The Executioner*],' Rothrock told *Fighter International* magazine in 1990. 'I think that if you have the right ingredients – the skill, the ability and the determination – no matter where you're from you can make it happen.'[9]

Shortly before her sixtieth birthday, Rothrock became the first practitioner of the martial arts to be awarded membership in the International Sports Hall of Fame (ISHOF), established to honour the achievements of outstanding sporting figures. She was inducted into the ISHOF by Arnold Schwarzenegger.

The female martial artist became a much sought-after personality by Hollywood cinema moguls from the 1970s onward. North Carolina-born Pam Grier began her martial arts training as a child and swiftly gained proficiency in karate, aikido, kung fu and jujitsu. The decision to learn fighting skills was in no small measure influenced by negative childhood experiences. Grier's family moved to Colorado when she was six years old and as a black girl in an overwhelmingly white society, she had to endure constant harassment at school. One day, three of her male classmates gave her a beating that left her traumatized, to the extent that she developed a stutter and would vanish from sight when friends came to visit her parents. Learning to defend herself against physical aggression was the key factor in overcoming the ordeals of her youth.

Grier has the distinction of being the only black American female skilled in martial arts to have made a splash on the big screen. Nearly a decade younger than Rothrock, she has to date appeared in more than twenty films throughout her career portrayed as a law enforcer and martial arts practitioner. Her fans saw her as a one-woman hit squad, thanks to her performances in action films like *Foxy Brown* (1974), in which she takes on villainous drug dealers, while giving the lie to the assumption that women are incapable of defeating a man in combat.

The United States by no means runs the show when it comes to female martial arts superstars. Taiwan gave the world an illustrious action film celebrity in the person of Angela Mao, 'Lady Kung Fu' to her fans, whose meteoric career kicked off, quite literally, at the age of seventeen when she was discovered by Hong Kong film director Huang Feng. Her early career as a child ballet and opera performer led to stardom in classics like *When Taekwondo Strikes* and *Enter the Dragon* (both 1973), which made use of her dazzling skills as a hapkido practitioner. What set Mao apart from most other Hong Kong film actors of the 1970s was her expertise as a hapkido black belt. Instead of acting out choreographed fight scenes, Mao's actual fighting skills exploded on the screen.

Publicity for another of her films to be released in 1973, *Deadly China Doll*, hails her as 'violent, unstoppable, unbreakable, dangerous and devastating'. She is also billed as 'delicious' in this film, which perhaps could be applied to the restaurants she opened in New York on her retirement after spending a decade battling her way through dozens of films. 'A lot happened to me in a little bit of time,' Mao said in a newspaper interview in 2016. 'I just played myself. I am strong and I am powerful. That is how I became the most important female Kung Fu actress of my time.'[10] Mao has been acclaimed as a radical feminist cinematic presence and even the Lauren Bacall of kung fu.

Of all American women to have made their mark in martial arts, surely one of the most inspirational and colourful has to be New Yorker Rena Glickman. A Brooklynite to her marrow, Glickman was born in Coney Island in 1935 to Jewish working-class parents who earned their living working a hot-dog stand on the boardwalk. Rena herself worked various jobs from the age of seven, which included helping out at the family business by peeling potatoes and selling cups of ice water after school. It was Glickman's tough upbringing that led her onto the path of street violence, when as a young girl she became leader of a notorious Brooklyn girls' gang called the Apaches.

One day, a family friend showed Glickman a move he had learned in a YMCA judo class. He was a good deal bigger and heavier than her and she suddenly found herself flipped over her friend's back, lying flat on the floor. That decided it, so more by chance than design Glickman joined a local judo club. At first, the YMCA instructor refused to accept her, as the class was for men only. But she was relentless, until finally she was permitted to attend the class.

This marked the starting point of a martial arts career as spectacular as it was unconventional. The self-control and mental calm that she had acquired early in her judo classes eventually drew her away from the rough-and-tumble life of gang warfare. But it was abruptly put to the test the day she was barred from a neighbourhood competition that did not accept women participants. For Glickman, whose mother had bestowed on her the nickname of 'Rusty', after a beloved local stray dog, the solution was simple: she would enter the competition disguised as a man.

In 1959 she put her name down for a YMCA championship in Upstate New York. On the day of the match, Rena strode into the gym with her hair trimmed short and her breasts flattened to her chest with masking tape. Her male opponent on that day stood little chance against this fierce opponent, who was unknown to the local judo community. He was soundly defeated in the ring.

When it came to handing out the awards, someone whispered into a judge's ear that he had seen Rena stripping off her uniform in a storeroom instead of the men's changing room. The judge bluntly asker Rena if she was a woman. She nodded and was immediately told to return her medal. From that day, Rena became ceaseless in her labours to put women on an equal footing in martial arts.

In 1962 Glickman travelled to Japan, where she made history as the first woman to train at the Kodokan global judo headquarters in Tokyo. There she met the judo and karate champion Ryohei Kanokogi. Two years later Rena Glickman became Rena 'Rusty' Kanokogi and the couple returned to the United States, where Ryohei launched his career as a judo pioneer in New York. Rusty was now more determined than ever to defy the widespread prejudices that existed against women participating in martial arts.

By 1980 she had persuaded New York's Madison Square Garden to host the first women's judo world championship and she also fought to introduce judo for women in the 1988 Seoul Summer Olympics. This was the same year in which she served as coach of the first U.S. Olympic women's judo team. Until her death in 2009, Rena carried on as a judo coach in Brooklyn, where she instructed a wide variety of students, from young children to U.S. marshals.

'Our boys and girls practise together,' she said. 'If one of the boys says, "Hey, you're losing to a girl", I call time out and ask, "What am I, a light bulb?" People always said judo wasn't feminine. I always said, "Tell that to my three kids".'[11]

Rusty's final honour was awarded posthumously, when in 2019 a ceremony was held in Brooklyn to mark the naming of a street 'Rena "Rusty" Kanokogi Way', with her family, disciples and members of the U.S. judo community in attendance to celebrate this mould-breaker's lifelong battle against discrimination towards women in martial arts.

Gender was not the only handicap that women martial artists had to contend with in those days. In November 1982 a federal judge in Boston ordered the U.S. National Karate Team to reinstate a top-ranked female competitor, 25-year-old Pam Glaser, who missed try-outs for the world championships because of a conflict with a Jewish holiday, Rosh Hashanah. The team was headed for the world competition in Taiwan that month. Judge Rya Zobel of the United States District Court said the national team had to accept the 1.5 metres (4 ft 11 in.) Glaser, who was the country's five-time women's kata, or patterns of movement, champion. The American Jewish Congress office in Boston filed a suit that led to the judge's decision that stated that Miss Glaser must be 'a full participating member'. A New York District Court was to hear a similar complaint from Lea Sukenik, a Jewish woman who was a nine-time member of the U.S. team and also missed the try-outs.[12]

IN CONTEMPORARY SOCIETY, WOMEN have in increasing numbers sought ways to help defend themselves against physical threats. The rate of abuse, verbal as well as actual violence, has soared in recent times, but the problem can be traced back many years. A 1977 issue of the British feminist magazine *Spare Rib* speaks of the threats and intimidation experienced by a woman named Alison Fell, in a series of confrontations that she faced while on her way home one night from London's Euston Station.

> A man was coming in the opposite direction. He made smacking, kissing noises . . . Immediately a light-coloured saloon veered in from the middle lane and slowed . . . I walked faster . . . 'Wanna lift, babe,' he slurred. I started to walk faster and faster. I was beginning to pant with terror and disgust. But still he caught up with me and muttered something in that vile prowler's hiss. Meanwhile, another man was crossing the road towards me.

To top off her night of dread and repulsion, Fell hailed a taxi to take her home and when she arrived at her door and was searching her bag for cash, the driver said, 'You wouldn't thinking of putting the coffee pot on for me, now love?'[13]

After making the point more than half a century ago that the majority of aggression against women takes place in the home rather than in public, *Spare Rib* raises the question of whether women should be organizing themselves against what is termed a generally violent society. Female karate students were asked if they thought learning self-defence had helped to reduce their fears. 'Today more young working women are coming to our classes, though we are still a minority,' one karate green belt was quoted as saying. 'Women seem to be treated with greater care in class, even though they are almost always more motivated to learn self-defence,' said Pauline Fuller, at that time a karate instructor at Women's Free Arts Alliance.

She believed women should be pushed just as hard as men to force out their latent aggression. 'I used to think women were naturally less aggressive than men, but this is no longer the case,' she says. 'In my class I don't even let them rest when they are tired. However, if faced with physical violence, I would still urge them to get away as quickly as possible.'[14] This position is in line with the central philosophy of karate and most other martial arts, that you gradually rid yourself of your ego and that part of you that wants to stand and fight to prove you're stronger than your opponent.

Rachel Lockton, director of Krav Maga Institute in New York City, says there has always been a significant proportion of women students at the school. 'Our membership is made up of at least one third and perhaps half women,' she says.

> I credit this to our communal ethos and focus on practical self-defence. That being said, whenever there is an increase in crime or danger or even in the media coverage of that danger, we see an uptick across the board and women are no different. We have found that at times when certain crime waves may be more targeted to them, there is an increase in inquiries from women.

Lockton points out that most people come to the dojo to learn a skill, gain confidence and be part of a community of like-minded people. This applies equally to women, who sign up to learn self-defence skills, quite often with fitness as a secondary motivation. In her view, Krav Maga displays clear differences with most other martial arts. 'It is inherently scalable and practical so that anyone of any age, size, gender or body type can wield the techniques effectively,' she says. 'It has been developed so that someone smaller and weaker can defend him or herself against someone larger and stronger.'

Lockton says situations have arisen in which women have had no alternative but to put their skills into practice.

> However, one of the primary shifts in mindset that we try to train and, which usually comes naturally after a student has been practising, is confidence and decision-making. This can manifest itself in a student having the instinct that something is wrong and feeling the confidence to act on it instead of taking a polite and compliant position. To be able to assess a situation, decide it is unsafe and take the proper steps to leave the situation, is just as important as any defence tactic.[15]

Community centres and martial arts studios that offer self-defence classes have seen interest soar since the 2024 U.S. presidential election. Within a week of Donald Trump's victory, which many feared would bring social instability and possible outbreaks of violence, the Krav Maga Institute received double their usual amount of course applications. A fortnight later, that figure had trebled. The sharp increase in numbers was not the only notable factor in these applications. The institute reported a significant influx of women joining the classes. There had traditionally been a 60:40 split in favour of men. That has now shifted to about 65 per cent women and 35 per cent men.

Heidi Eggleton, an assistant psychologist working in Britain's NHS, has more than fifteen years of martial arts experience and has developed a trauma-informed karate programme for victims of abuse. She has also founded a girls' and women's karate club in Dorset, southwest England. According to an article in 2024 by Eggleton on the link between participation in martial arts and psychological well-being, martial arts ideally 'are built on a foundation of respect, control and discipline, [but] they can often simultaneously foster a hegemonic masculine environment composed of egos, athleticism and competence biases'.

Eggleton says that a key influence in women's increased participation in martial arts has been the promotion of equality between the sexes, or gender mainstreaming as it is known. This has become evident in innovative events like the introduction of women's boxing in the 2012 Olympic Games, which increases opportunities for participation by women and girls.

> [It was] found that mixed-gender training can challenge sexist interpretations of women's bodies and provide women with the opportunity to be equal and mutually respected by men. On the other hand [...] mixed-gender training can be problematic. One reason for this could be that men fear being overpowered by a woman, and consequently act more aggressively than necessary in mixed training encounters.[16]

It is evident from the foregoing that women hold a prevalent place in martial arts, irrespective of social rank, nationality or, for that matter, age. Meenakshi Raghavan, from Kerala in southern India, is an instructor of Kalarippayattu, one of the country's oldest martial arts, which traces its origins back at least 3,000 years to the Indus Valley civilization known as the Harappan civilization. Raghavan is 83 years old and continues to practise and instruct in Kalari – as the martial art is abbreviated – on a full-time basis. Raghavan has often expounded the healing and spiritual aspects of Kalari, with its holistic emphasis on self-defence and well-being. The town of Vadakara is where she trains and holds daily classes, from 5 a.m. until 12 p.m., for some fifty students, including her own four children. The syllabus follows a five-year progression, from learning fighting skills with different weapons to the highest pinnacle, which is mastery of unarmed combat. Raghavan says Kalari is gaining popularity, especially among children, who find it an approachable vehicle to self-esteem.

Chi Body instructor Mark Li says he has seen an increasing number of children as well as women joining his classes. 'For one thing, it serves as an escape valve for their great store of energy,' he says.

> They also come to understand that this is not only about physical activities. Martial arts should teach them goodness, to carry out even menial undertakings, like helping their parents with household chores. By fulfilling more of these tasks over time, they begin to understand why they should be doing them. Then they develop the willingness without their parents having to force them to do it. This same attitude carries over into martial arts.[17]

As an aside, it may be mentioned that the celebrated Japanese founder of judo, Yoshiaki Yamashita, was the instructor of a number of prominent U.S. women, among whom figure photographer Martha Blow Wadsworth, wife and mother of U.S. senators Hallie Elkins and her sister Grace Davis Lee. Blow Wadsworth was particularly well connected to the country's political elite. Fellow judo practitioner Theodore Roosevelt once paid her a visit to have photographs taken of his horse Roswell jumping over a stone wall.

The Shaolin Temple has its counterpart in north London, where in 2007 Master Shi Yan Gui, who trained at the Chinese temple, set up his academy to impart a modern approach to teaching traditional martial arts. Myrsini Chionia Christodoulelli, an award-winning martial artist in her own right, with years of experience in traditional

Shaolin kung fu, tai chi and Sanda (a fighting system that originated with the Chinese armed forces), is the academy's instructor of female-only and junior classes. She is also a stage and screen performer, who has acted and played lead roles in numerous films and theatre productions. Myrsini has represented Shaolin Temple Cultural Centre on numerous occasions in national and international events and is currently a member of Team GB Traditional Wushu Squad.

'From a young age, I developed a passion for Wushu kung fu, influenced by Bruce Lee's films and, later, Wuxia, a genre focusing on chivalry in martial arts,' she says.

> This includes films like *House of Flying Daggers* and *Crouching Tiger, Hidden Dragon*. However, in my small village near Athens, kung fu was unheard of and my parents could not afford to send me to any other sports classes. For me, kung fu encompassed my love of transformation, fighting ability, acrobatics, protecting your loved ones and, also, theatricality.[18]

When she moved to London to pursue her acting dream and attend drama school, Myrsini still yearned to learn the Wushu martial art known as Wushu kung fu, to be able to play roles in action films. Despite a demanding schedule and mental health struggles during her early years in London, she persisted in her dream to train. 'In drama school, I found the stage combat training limited and unsatisfying, as it didn't teach real fighting skills,' she says. 'I began searching for authentic kung fu schools but struggled to find one that met my standards. Finally, in 2017, I met Shifu Yan Gui and, after a long wait, I joined his school.'

Myrsini firmly believes that martial arts greatly enhance overall health and well-being, especially Chinese martial arts, taught by

Instructor Myrsini Chionia Christodoulelli at Shaolin Temple Martial Arts and Cultural Centre, London.

a real master who has undergone strict training and is recognized by the International Wushu Federation, the Shaolin Temple China or the Chinese Wushu Association. 'Unfortunately there are too many self-proclaimed "Masters" who have acquired their credentials online during the Covid lockdown and also started teaching online,' she says. 'It is sad that they have followers and people who believe whatever they sell them. I find this a sacrilege.'

Master Shi Yan Gui agrees that online instruction is not the path to follow to truly develop martial arts skills. 'Since the days of Covid, I've been thinking about the place of martial arts in today's world of AI and virtual reality,' he says. 'A lot of instructors carried on teaching online, which strikes me as more negative than positive. As a student you need the watchful eye of the instructor to guide and be with you. Online martial arts classes became more of a fitness experience.'[19]

Myrsini says that for women, martial arts are especially useful for building physical strength, mental resilience and self-confidence. 'They offer an opportunity to reclaim personal power, challenge societal norms about women's physicality and create a strong sense of achievement,' she says.

> In our area of London, which is disadvantaged and can be dangerous, many women come to learn self-defence, and they stay because they love the programme we've created for them. We offer a supportive, empowering environment that encourages growth at every level. Ultimately, the reasons people come and stay in martial arts will vary based on their needs, their location and the school they choose. But for women, it's a unique way to build strength and confidence in body and mind.[20]

Melanie D. Gibson, a taekwon-do black belt, would no doubt voice full agreement with Myrsini's acclaim of the benefits of martial arts training. She speaks of life-changing lessons that she acquired from her years of practise, in which she discovered a path to inner peace and a mode for her real self to emerge. As a young woman living in Fort Worth, Texas, Gibson found herself inconsolably depressed and trapped inside self-destructive thinking, 'cultivated by a lifetime of fear, doubt and self-loathing'.[21] She had taken taekwon-do lessons as a child of ten and developed a love for the discipline and the slow, meticulous metronome of progress in the art. Gibson stopped training at age twelve and, in her own words, lost herself for the next 22 years.

What followed were more than two decades of despair, turbulent relationships and general misery for reasons lacking in logical justification, but which can effectively hijack a person's state of mind and body. Then came the day Gibson decided to make a major positive change in her life: she would return to taekwon-do. 'All I knew at the time was that if I didn't get into the dojang and out of my addled, dangerous mind, I might end up dead,' she says.[22]

After taking up her first class, Gibson was certain that the dormant taekwon-do gene in her body was beginning to awaken. She moved steadily up the grades and simultaneously began to acquire a sense of self-esteem and an aura of confidence that took hold in her daily life. 'It was around this time that I began to really appreciate the mental and emotional stability my taekwon-do practice brought me,' she says.[23]

Gibson earned her much-coveted black belt, an event that, she stresses, placed her still at the beginning of a martial arts student's journey. She has since been awarded her 2nd Dan and is hard at work on training for her 3rd. Taekwon-do drew her out of what she describes as her 'hardened shell'. Gibson returned to taekwon-do when her mind and body finally grew weary of struggling. 'Oddly enough,' she says, 'kicking and screaming in taekwon-do class finally quietened the kicking and screaming inside my mind and soul.'[24]

Contemporary American and European women are not the only ones making their mark in martial arts. In the same way filmgoers might aspire to superhero fame, many Chinese women dream of becoming martial arts heroes. To fulfil this aspiration, the Emei Kung Fu Girls, a group of young Chinese women, have brought new passion to traditional Chinese martial arts and sparked a nationwide craze.

'In a promotional video released in early May [2024], nine group members demonstrated the signature weapons of the Emei Kung Fu Girls school with fluid movements and exquisite skills,' says *China Daily* reporter Huang Zhiling.

> The video they produced has received more than a billion views and is trending on Chinese social media platforms. Comments by netizens frequently liken them to heroes out of Chinese martial arts novels. 'We didn't expect to receive so much attention and love right after our debut,' says Ma-Zhao Lingyun, a core member of the group. The compliments and encouragement are an honour and inspire us to make more progress in inheriting and promoting Emei Kung Fu and traditional Chinese culture.[25]

As an inheritor of Emei Kung Fu, Lingyun rose to Internet fame in 2020 in a video in which she tosses a sword into the air and wields it with blinding swiftness in a series of Emei moves. All this while taking out the morning rubbish. 'Through the Emei Kung Fu Girls – the first female martial arts intellectual property to go viral in China . . . Lingyun hopes to lead more young people to appreciate traditional culture.' She is not satisfied with simply being an ordinary idol group and strives to make breakthroughs in cultural innovation and expression.[26] Li Jieyu, who manages the group, said members of the Emei Kung Fu Girls receive daily training on Emei Mountain in Sichuan province from inheritors of Emei school martial arts. In addition to learning basic skills and characteristic Emei moves, they follow specialized training courses, including riding, archery and performing arts to improve their performances on stage.

Li Nuofei, another member, said that she enjoys the strength and beauty that come with martial arts, despite the exhausting training. She noted that perseverance and patience are the keys to learning the skills. She says the group wishes to exchange ideas with international martial arts practitioners, as well as with different regional cultures around the world, to create new works in different forms, including short plays, flash mobs and variety shows.

Emei martial arts boast a history of nearly 3,000 years and provides a solid foundation for the popularity of the Emei Kung Fu Girls. By blending martial arts with other cultural elements, such as dance, music and costumes, the Emei Kung Fu Girls exhibit a strong sense of modernity and fashion. Wang Chao, a national-level inheritor of Emei martial arts, said people have been flocking to Emei Mountain to study kung fu in recent years, especially after the Emei Kung Fu Girls made a name for themselves around the country. Let it never be said that women, now as in the past, do not play a prominent role in martial arts.

4

LIGHTS, CAMERA, ACTION!

On a steamy morning, 23 July 1973, a cordon of more than two hundred Hong Kong policemen stood with locked arms, struggling to hold back a crowd of thousands of sobbing mourners who had come to attend the funeral service for their beloved Chinese-American kung fu idol. Bruce Lee, the world's first Asian superstar, had died of cerebral oedema the previous week at the age of 32. His death was believed to have been caused by an overdose of painkillers. In the Buddhist service, Lee's body was dressed in black-coloured Chinese pyjamas, similar to those worn in his 1972 film *Fist of Fury*. The grandeur of the occasion in the British colony rivalled that of a state funeral. The memorial service at the Kowloon Funeral Parlour was attended by no fewer than five hundred VIPs bereaved dressed in white, the Chinese colour of mourning. 'Seeing his hearse begin to depart, Bruce's fans went wild with grief,' reported Lee's biographer Matthew Polly. 'Many mourners refused to leave because they knew this was the last time they would be near their hero.'[1]

As we've seen, female celebrities are by no means absent from the roster of skilled martial arts practitioners worldwide. Scarlett Johansson is another Hollywood star who was obliged to acquire martial arts skills for a role, in this case as 'Black Widow', a member of the ensemble of heroes in the Avengers film series and the focus of the 2021 superhero film *Black Widow* by Marvel Studios. Natasha Romanoff, known by her alias 'Black Widow', is a former Russian spy, who from early childhood is tutored in bareknuckle combat, training in jujitsu, judo and Muay Thai. Johansson worked out on the set with her co-star Jeremy Renner, who also had to deploy his own skills as a non-superhero character, Hawkeye. Johansson's experiences converted her into a devotee of jujitsu, an enthusiasm she shares with screenwriter and co-star Robert Downey Jr, who gained proficiency in the martial art for the Guy Ritchie-directed Sherlock Holmes film franchise. Johansson has since continued her training with Brazilian-American martial arts instructor Rigan Machado.

Showbusiness is not the only profession that has given the world talented martial artists. French model and actress Laetitia Casta, who has featured on more than eighty magazine covers in her career, is a familiar face on adverts for L'Oréal, Dior and Chanel. What is less known about this supermodel is that she holds a brown belt in judo, which she has been practising since childhood. In Turkey, Miss World 2002 beauty queen Azra Akin displayed her judo skills the following year with her first-place win in the British reality sports TV series *The Games*. Another major name in the modelling world, the Oxford-born Yasmin Le Bon, regularly practises judo with her husband Simon Le Bon, the lead singer of pop group Duran Duran, at London's Budokwai. This venerable martial arts centre was opened more than a century ago by Japanese master Gunji Koizumi, considered to be the founding father of judo in Britain. International media magnets from Bruce Lee to Elvis Presley, as I discuss later in this chapter, played an instrumental role in the twentieth century in catapulting martial arts from an esoteric pursuit involving a relatively small elite of followers to a global activity on a par with Big Business in terms of revenue.

The worldwide value of the martial arts industry currently stands at around $90 billion and is forecast to nearly double to $171 billion by 2028. Of the countries with the greatest percentage of martial arts followers, the United States is the most diligent in compiling statistics. There are more than 42,000 martial arts schools in America, employing around 70,000 people and giving instruction to some 18 million students, of which roughly half are adults and the rest teenagers and children. The average martial arts student in the United States is 33 years old, although children between six and twelve make up the largest age group. The gender demographics show that 60 per cent of people currently enrolled in martial arts classes are men.[2]

In Britain, more than 900,000 adults regularly attend martial arts classes and enrolments continue to grow each year. Taekwon-do, karate and judo are the three most popular disciplines among young people, as is also the case for children in the five- to ten-year-old range. Karate and taekwon-do also figure as the most widely followed martial arts among women, with judo lagging behind in third place.

In Japan, while reliable numbers are not easy to obtain, karate is believed to have 3 million adherents, followed by aikido with an estimated 1 million and judo with around 120,000. Shorinji Kempo, a Japanese martial art with roots in Chinese kung fu and jujitsu lag behind with some 70,000 practitioners in both disciplines. China, on the other hand, the birthplace of some of the most popular traditional martial arts, attracts a smaller fraction of its population than might be expected. Karate was not known in China until its introduction in 1990 and gained a measure of official recognition nearly twenty years later. There are at present some 20,000 karate schools operating across the country. As for kung fu, so intrinsically linked with China, this discipline has for decades enjoyed a solid influence on the entertainment world but, contrary to popular perception, its practice among the general workaday Chinese people is relatively insignificant.

On a global scale, it is estimated that more than 100 million people are involved in modern and traditional martial arts. Why do they do it? What are the physical and emotive drivers? The answers will vary according to age group, gender and personal circumstances. The most commonly cited aims are for the acquisition of sporting skills, the desire to learn self-defence techniques and the need to build self-esteem. Karate black belt Joe Hyams, a former war correspondent and disciple of such luminaries as Ed Parker and Bruce Lee, maintained that the martial arts are essentially avenues through which 'the true master can achieve spiritual serenity, mental tranquillity and the deepest self-confidence.'[3]

Taekwon-do Grandmaster Donato Nardizzi explains that in addition to physical development, character building and self-defence skills, which hold essential value in any context, the practice of the martial art that he has chosen in today's society provides a valuable alternative to screen time by offering a disciplined activity that promotes physical movement, real-world interaction and mental concentration. 'Taekwon-do builds authentic self-esteem through earned accomplishments instead of superficial social media validation in a world where superficiality dominates,' he says. 'The mindfulness training in taekwon-do helps students develop mental clarity and resilience by providing a necessary balance against the fast-paced, information-rich environment of our modern world. Taekwon-do serves as a lifelong practice which teaches people to succeed in their bodies and minds while enduring any social challenges they encounter.'[4]

Donato Nardizzi demonstrating a knife-hand guarding block.

Bruce Lee's death came only a few weeks after the premiere of his legendary film *Enter the Dragon*, which tragically he never got to see. It was his first motion picture to draw worldwide acclaim. The film grossed more than $400 million, equivalent to an estimated $2 billion today adjusted for inflation, making it one of the most profitable in cinema history at the time. *Enter the Dragon* remains unchallenged as the most successful martial arts film to hit the screens. The plot revolves around Lee's recruitment by British Intelligence as an undercover agent to track down the notorious crime boss Han, a sinister megalomaniac who is running a martial arts tournament and is suspected of involvement in drugs and prostitution. Lee plays a Shaolin master who enters the competition. He is a man of monkish purity and spirituality, but in possession of a laser-like focus on exposing and eventually putting Han, in no uncertain terms, out of the picture. Lee's most successful cinema undertaking may have been one of the chief factors that led to his early death. Lee's biographer

Bruce Lee in a scene from *Enter the Dragon* (1973, dir. Robert Clouse).

Matthew Polly says that according to the kung fu's star's wife Linda, Lee was sleep-deprived due to the stress of filming *Enter the Dragon*, which had drained him physically and mentally. 'He had lost fifteen per cent of his total body weight in the previous two months and he had minimal body fat to start,' he says. 'If Bruce Lee's collapse was the result of heat stroke, then the doctors misdiagnosed him. They caught the post-cooling complication of cerebral oedema but didn't grasp or treat its cause.'[5]

'From 1974 through to the end of the decade, nearly all martial arts magazines in the U.S. contained ads for coloured T-shirts with a cartoon illustration of Lee's image and the wishful proclamation "Bruce Lee Lives"', notes historian Davis Miller.[6] July 1973 denoted something more profound than the passing of an action film hero. Bruce Lee's short life placed martial arts centre stage across the world, in particular in the United States, and symbolized an awakening – the popularization and glamourization, if one can forgive the hackneyed expressions, of martial arts for the many millions of followers who took up one or another of these fighting skills. These practices of course included Lee's own school of combat. The inscription that Lee's American wife Linda chose for his gravestone reads, 'Founder of Jeet Kune Do'.

Lee had begun to train in martial arts before he left his native Hong Kong at eighteen to take up residence in the United States. He was sent to America by his parents, who were worried about their son's frequent involvement in street brawls and the occasional conflict with the Hong Kong police. This early life of insecurity and confrontation encouraged Lee to seek ways to explore his inner self, aiming to develop personal self-esteem and confidence. He initially took up Wing Chung, a system of self-defence based on a southern Chinese version of kung fu. Lee then went on to study various styles of martial arts and their related philosophies, selecting from each discipline the teachings he considered to be most relevant to his life. The result was the conception of Jeet Kune Do, which translates as 'the way of the intercepting fist', a system infused with meditative as well as fighting techniques. This discipline was strongly influenced by Western boxing, wrestling and fencing and manifests a contemporary image in its rejection of sterile tradition, focusing instead on efficiency and practical effectiveness.

The motion picture industry had been producing martial arts films long before Bruce Lee burst onto the international screen with his first major lead role, as Cheng Chao-an in *The Big Boss* (1971), which in its U.S. showing was originally titled *Fist of Fury*. The phenomenon can be traced back more than four decades before Lee's debut: the pioneering kung fu action film *The Burning of the Red Lotus Temple* (1928), a Chinese silent film that can truly lay claim to being the first of the genre. It was a groundbreaking saga about a band of fighters who deploy their martial arts skills to defend the clan's holy sanctuary from marauders.

Bruce Lee's launch as a martial arts name to fans in the United States, which became his primary public, came in 1966 when he co-starred as Kato in *The Green Hornet*, a television detective series, with Van Williams in the starring role, adapted from a radio series and comic. 'American audiences may have shrugged at *The Green Hornet*, but [it] was adored by the martial arts community, who claimed Bruce Lee as its first breakout star,' says Polly.[7]

Early in 1971 a New York theatre premiered America's first look at a Chinese martial arts film, *Five Fingers of Death*. In that same year in Chicago, a second Chinese and no less flamboyant action film, *Duel of the Iron Fist*, made its debut. 'With the release of Bruce Lee's films, the market exploded,' note the authors of *The Encyclopedia of Martial Arts Movies*. 'Most people love to watch gymnastics during the Olympics but fail to see the similarities between those athletes and the martial artists starring in these films . . . Both are exciting to watch and fill the viewer with a feeling of exhilaration.'[8]

Enter the Dragon was released in Hong Kong on 26 July 1973, six days after Lee's death. Director Robert Clouse, who was well-known for his work in the field of action films, brought in several big names to co-star alongside Lee. Jackie Chan, who was to gain international fame as a martial arts legend in his day, made a brief onscreen appearance in *Enter the Dragon* as a stuntman. The established U.S. actor John Saxon, who had acquired some experience in martial arts, provides assistance in the story, as does Jim Kelly, best known as an American athlete who dabbled in martial arts. Shih Kien offers a memorable performance as Han, the criminal mastermind. Kien was a Hong Kong actor and martial artist who brought many years of experience to the narrative. He usually featured as the bad guy in Hong Kong films, dating back to the black-and-white era. In *Enter the Dragon*, martial arts dominate the screen as never in the past. The action scenes easily eclipse an unremarkable and somewhat hackneyed plot. However, in making its debut in the American market, the Hong Kong kung fu film industry triggered something of a cultural transformation in the United States, clearly demonstrated in the massive box-office success of *Enter the Dragon*.

'Furthermore, as has been widely acknowledged by cultural critics, Bruce Lee's heroic persona regenerated a sense of pride for ethnic Chinese everywhere,' says author and martial arts historian Paul Bowman. At the very least, after Bruce Lee, Asians in the West were no longer automatically represented through entirely negative stereotypes. Of course, what Bruce Lee offered was also a stereotype. 'But,' Bowman points out, 'as stereotypes go, being tarred with the image of the invincible, disciplined, ethical hero who champions China and fights for justice, is perhaps not too bad a deal.'[9]

Towards the end of the film, Lee takes on one of the minor villains from the gang in a battle inside a cave and quickly dispatches him by breaking his neck in a stranglehold. Had Lee known who his cinema adversary was destined to become in real life, he might well

Celebrated martial artist and film star Jackie Chan, 1996.

have been thinking, *Don't even imagine you're going to steal my thunder, you interloper.* His victim was none other than Jackie Chan, who the *New York Times* once extolled in a biographical piece as 'the undisputed king of the Asian screen, the inheritor of Bruce Lee's mantle, a martial artist whose numerous films hold box office records throughout Asia.'[10]

Jackie Chan's exploits on the big screen gave a huge boost to people's awareness of martial arts and indeed many thousands of inspired spectators began to fill the dojos of karate and kung fu academies, not only in the United States but across the world. Chan shot to fame as the unrivalled martial arts star of his day, a man who struck terror into the hearts of his enemies and could see off all comers with deadly punches and kicks. Chan was less successful in dealing with his fans: namely, the hordes of young Asian women who thronged his offices every morning to catch a glimpse of their idol. American actors who featured in his films paled into insignificance compared with the amount of attention lavished on Chan, to the extent that on at least two occasions, neglected female devotees attempted to commit suicide in his hallway.

Chan's great moment came in 1980, at the age of 26, with his first starring role in the U.S. motion picture *The Big Brawl*, also released as *Battle Creek Brawl*. Directed by American filmmaker Robert Clouse, it included much of the crew from *Enter the Dragon*. The action takes place mostly in the crime-ridden streets of Chicago in the 1930s. Chan plays the part of a Chinese American martial artist who throws down the gauntlet to the Mafia, capped by an unrestrained street battle culminating in a desperate fight for survival. Here we see the raw substance of Jackie Chan transposed to the Tinseltown screen, a slapstick martial arts comedy saturated with acrobatic and innovative stunts executed with supreme expertise by

Chan himself. Where Bruce Lee came to symbolize deadly serious, no-nonsense martial warfare, Chan injected a helping of comedy into his fight scenes and it is quite common to find the protagonist getting a laugh out of his own capers.

A martial arts film that has undergone several reincarnations over the past forty-odd years is the 1984 John G. Avildsen-directed hit *The Karate Kid*. It was an enormous success in terms of revenue, grossing $100 million in the United States and Canada. The franchise features Ralph Macchio as Daniel LaRusso in four versions of *The Karate Kid*. The plot of the first film revolves around LaRusso, who moves from New Jersey to Los Angeles, where he finds himself the victim of bullying by Johnny Lawrence, the ex-boyfriend of LaRusso's flame Ali Mills. To defend himself, LaRusso takes up karate and eventually achieves a high level of expertise that allows him to compete in a tournament. The fifth film, released in 2010, affirms its martial arts credentials with Jackie Chan in the lead role. The plot was created by Robert Mark Kamen, who scripted the first three films in the series. The story also involves a family move, this time to Beijing, where twelve-year-old Dre Parker is viciously attacked by bullies until kung fu master Mr Han, played by Jackie Chan, intervenes on the boy's behalf. The sixth film in the franchise, titled *The Karate Kid: Legends*, was released in cinemas in 2025, with Jackie Chan, now 71 and in fit fighting form, Ralph Macchio and Ben Wang in the lead roles. Wang plays Li Fong, a kung fu prodigy and Chinese student taken to New York by his mother. There, Li struggles to fit in with his new classmates. He eventually enters a karate competition but his limited skills hold him back. In steps, Jackie Chan and the omnipresent Daniel LaRusso teach him to merge his diverse skills into one for the ultimate martial arts showdown.

ANY MENTION OF HIGH-PROFILE personalities in the world of martial arts must take into account that before Bruce Lee, Jackie Chan and the other immortals of the silver screen, there was the 26th president of the United States, Theodore Roosevelt.

'I was a sickly, delicate boy, suffered much from asthma and frequently had to be taken away on trips to find a place where I could breathe,' Roosevelt says in his autobiography. He writes later on, 'Having been a sickly boy, with no natural bodily prowess and having lived much at home, I was at first quite unable to hold my own when thrown into contact with other boys of rougher antecedents.'[11] This autobiographic portrayal of a frail youth, who also endured regular bullying at school, hardly conforms to the celebrated image of Teddy Roosevelt the Rough Rider, brandishing his sword as he leads the charge on horseback up San Juan Hill in the Spanish–American War of 1898.

Roosevelt began taking steps to overcome his physical weaknesses as early as 1876. In that year he entered Harvard University, where he would occasionally compete in wrestling and boxing tournaments. This was the lead-up to his martial arts training, which started in the early 1900s with judo instruction, when Roosevelt was already well into his forties and in his first term as president after serving as Governor of New York State. He developed a deep enthusiasm for the Japanese martial art, which satisfied his craving for fighting competitions. He would occasionally take time out from his chores in the Oval Office to organize sparring matches in the White House basement, at times with opponents who even included members of his own family.

The person who introduced Roosevelt to judo was Yoshiaki Yamashita, a distinguished Japanese martial artist with impeccable credentials, having been the disciple of Jigoro Kano, considered the

'Washington item: Mr. Roosevelt is taking wrestling lessons from a Japanese instructor', 26 March 1904.

founder of the art. Author Joseph R. Svinth wrote in a magazine article, 'The President's training partners included his sons, his private secretary, the Japanese naval attaché, Secretary of War William Howard Taft and Secretary of the Interior Gifford Pinchot. When these people were unavailable, then Roosevelt tried tricks on muscular young visitors.'[12]

Teddy Roosevelt was the first but by no means the only world leader to embrace a martial art. Apart from the aforementioned Vladimir Putin, Canada's charismatic Pierre Trudeau received his judo black belt on a visit to Japan in 1970. Trudeau, who served as prime minister for fifteen years, began his training in judo in the 1950s, when the art was beginning to gain popularity in his country. Historian Paul Nurse wrote an article titled *Pierre Trudeau and Judo* in an Ontario magazine, in which he explains:

> Following the end of the Second World War and the relocation of many Japanese-Canadians to Canada's eastern regions,

Jigoro Kano and celebrated Japanese judoka Kyuzo Mifune, before 1938.

> judo likewise emigrated east—first to Alberta, then Quebec, Ontario and the maritime provinces. This period saw the establishment of such legendary facilities as Toronto's Kidokwan, Hatashita and Montreal's Shidokan Seidokwan judo clubs.[13]

The 1950s witnessed the arrival of more than a few European judo and jujitsu instructors in North America. Of those who established their new homes in Canada, quite a few settled in Quebec, where they fomented the spread of Japanese combative systems. When judo began to attract followers in Trudeau's hometown of Montreal, he was at once interested by what it had to offer physically and spiritually. 'This postwar situation was made to order for Trudeau, who had returned from his celebrated round-the-world journey of 1948–9 with a marked taste for the exotic and an affinity for Eastern ways and modes of thinking,' Nurse says. 'Interested also in Buddhism, Trudeau trained regularly throughout the rest of the 1950s and managed to earn a brown belt by the end of the decade. In the early 1960s, he took some time to visit the famed Kodokan (Judo Institute) during a trip to Tokyo.'[14] Trudeau was awarded his black belt in 1970, on a return visit to Japan. The impact he made on his homeland as well as Canadian judo can be felt to this day. It is estimated that more than 4,000 Canadians are now training in judo, most of whom are members of clubs affiliated with the Canadian Kokokwan Black Belt Association. Many of these practitioners are women and one Toronto secretary, Elaine McCrossan, in 1959 became the first Canadian woman to be promoted to black belt. In 2013 the Canadian Black Belt Hall of Fame acknowledged his contribution to judo by creating the Pierre Elliott Trudeau Humanitarian Award.

Like father, like son. Justin Trudeau's father Pierre encouraged his eldest son, who served two terms as Canadian prime minister from

Illustration printed in a late 19th-century French dictionary depicting some moves of the Japanese martial art of jujitsu.

2015 to 2025, to take up the martial art from an early age and sent him to train at the Takahashi Dojo in Ottawa. The tradition has carried on to a third generation of judokas, with Justin Trudeau's son and daughter also attending classes at the celebrated Canadian dojo.

The list of personalities who have taken up martial arts throughout modern history reads like a roll-call of eminent politicians and renowned celebrities, numbering in their hundreds. Starting with U.S. presidents, the register is extensive and, likewise, contains a few surprises. Mention the name George Washington and what comes to mind is the image of a muscular, avuncular eighteenth-century American statesman and military commander wearing a powdered wig. That would have been an accurate picture in later life, when he was leading the Continental Army against British colonial forces in the American War of Independence. Much earlier, however, when Washington was in his mid-teens, he attended boarding school at

Virginia's Rev. Maury's Academy. As a spindly lad, Washington often had to endure the humiliation of being pushed around the school yard by bullying classmates. He soon took the decision to learn to act in his own defence by training in wrestling. While not a martial art in the strictest sense, the Irish wrestling style he took up used throws, kicks, locks and even chokes, all of which are techniques brought into play in some of the classic disciplines. Washington's innate fighting spirit enabled him to give the school bullies a taste of their own medicine and turned the first U.S. President into a wrestling champion.

Towering over his compatriots at 2 metres (6 ft 4 in.), the very sight of Abraham Lincoln would serve to dishearten even the most belligerent of bullies. To impress upon his adversaries that the future sixteenth president of the United States was not a man to be trifled with and following in the footsteps of Washington, Lincoln took up a school of fighting known as 'collar and elbow' wrestling. In its simplest form, this entailed placing a hand behind a foe's neck and the other behind his elbow, to throw the opponent swiftly to the floor.

As a young man, Lincoln would often indulge in a catch-as-catch-can grappler. In the years he spent in New Salem, Illinois, Lincoln had occasion to confront a local gang of ruffians and free-for-all street fighters known as the Clary's Grove Boys. The gang's habitual terrorizing of New Salem came to a crashing end in 1831, when the 22-year-old Lincoln was asked by the townspeople to take on the gang leader Jack Armstrong. He did so and mercilessly beat the lout into submission. Lincoln was always on the lookout for bullies, even when he was on the campaign trail for his election to the White House. During an outdoor rally, he spotted a supporter in the crowd being pushed about by a heckler. Lincoln strutted down from the podium, grabbed the troublemaker, hurled him into the air and climbed back onto the platform to resume his speech.[15]

The number of American presidents with a penchant for free-for-all-style wrestling carries on across party lines. After leading the Union Army to victory in the U.S. Civil War, General Ulysses S. Grant, who was to become the eighteenth president of the United States, decided he was obliged to apologize to his adversary, General Robert E. Lee, for the sorry state in which he found the area where the peace treaty was signed. As Grant explained to the Confederate leader, the previous evening he and some of his fellow officers had indulged in a night of wrestling in camp.

Boxing and wrestling have attracted a number of U.S. Presidents in the twentieth century. Howard Taft became a wrestling champion while an undergraduate at Yale University; Dwight Eisenhower engaged in boxing as well as wrestling; and Gerald Ford was a boxing coach at Yale and also in the U.S. Navy.

Once traditional martial arts had been established in the United States and were gaining in popularity, several more American leaders began taking an interest in one or another of the classic disciplines. Bill Clinton was already approaching middle age when he began to dabble in taekwon-do. In 1987 the 41-year-old Governor of Arkansas received his honorary black belt from Songahm, America's largest association teaching the Korean martial art. In fact, the future president arranged for the World Championships to be held in Little Rock, the state capital of Arkansas. Officially, Clinton was not a dedicated practitioner, but in 2001, near the end of his term of office as president, he was awarded an honorary 9th Dan by the World Taekwondo headquarters in South Korea.

Barack Obama was very much a devoted taekwon-do enthusiast before and during his years in the White House, eventually rising to the level of green belt. Obama's association with martial arts goes back to his childhood, part of which was spent in Indonesia, where he took up Pencak Silat. This traditional style of fighting taught him to deploy his full body to deliver strikes, grappling and throwing techniques, many of which he would later perfect when he began to study taekwon-do.

Early in his career, as instructor in constitutional law at the University of Chicago from 1992 to 2004, Obama began training in the martial art under David Posner, a financial capital planner and taekwon-do instructor who acclaimed his former student as 'very disciplined, very diligent, with phenomenal balance and very good foot work, along with really good solid stances'.[16]

Obama's years of taekwon-do training came to the fore in his approach to decision-making, reflected in the clear stress he placed on carefully executed responses to political challenges, at home and abroad. What comes through from Obama's taekwon-do practice during his eight years in the White House is the weight he placed on discipline and focus. It was during his first term of office that Obama the showman displayed his martial arts skills to President Lee Myung-Bak, on a state visit to South Korea. This came about during a ceremony at the presidential palace in Seoul, when during a break in their summit talks Lee bestowed on his American counterpart an honorary taekwon-do black belt.[17]

The United States does not hold the exclusive claim on heads of state who have demonstrated an enthusiasm for martial arts. Spain's former king Juan Carlos obtained his black belt in taekwon-do in 1962 when he was prince of Spain and would engage in sparring sessions with his brother-in-law, the future King Constantine II of Greece. There is a famous photo of the two princes in combat the day before Juan Carlos's marriage to Princess Sofía. It was a painful ceremony for Juan Carlos, who suffered a fractured collarbone in the match.

Taekwon-do fighter breaking a wooden board during training.

Xi Jinping, who has served as president of the People's Republic of China since 2013, while not known to be a martial artist in his own right, has used these disciplines as part of his 'pop culture' drive to bolster his personal profile. Xi's soft power policies came to the fore a year after taking office, when the Chinese leader was photographed, bow and arrow held aloft, at a Sino-Mongolian summit. The symbolism of this act was interpreted as an allusion to the fictional Chinese martial arts hero Guo Ling, the protagonist of novelist Jin Yong's epic *The Eagle-Shooting Heroes* (a parody of *The Legend of the Condor Heroes*). Yong's book is celebrated throughout China as a classic tale of Wuxia, an expression meaning the 'chivalrous martial arts' of ancient China. Archery, along with kung fu, is one of the skills in which Guo Ling excels and puts to use in the defence of his Chinese compatriots. In 1993 the book was adapted as a Hong Kong comedy film directed by Jeffrey Lau, who gained fame writing and directing slapstick movies known as *mo lei tau* comedies.

IT WILL HARDLY COME AS A SURPRISE that more than any other country, America has provided the greatest number of celebrities with an attachment to martial arts. Some of these personalities, past and present, rank among the most renowned stars of stage and screen. Curiously, while contemporary U.S. presidents have displayed a partiality for acquiring taekwon-do skills, Hollywood stars have shown more of a predilection for judo.

James Cagney was renowned for his tough-guy roles, in which he excelled thanks in no small measure to his judo schooling. Cagney, who rose to black belt, spent years training under Kenneth Kuniyuki, one of America's top twentieth-century judo instructors. His fighting ability served him well in films like *G Men*, one of the top-grossing films of 1935 as well being a classic depiction of martial arts on the big screen. In the film, Cagney plays an FBI agent who sets out to take revenge for the gangster murder of a friend. His induction into the U.S. law enforcement agency includes self-defence instruction in boxing and judo. Cagney did not treat cinemagoers to a display of his martial arts abilities until a decade later, with the 1945 release of *Blood on the Sun*, in which the actor displays his judo techniques in a clash with Japanese warmongers. This culminates in a ferocious battle, with Cagney beating to a pulp the gangland leader with a volley of kicks and throws. It can be said that with the release of *Blood on the Sun*, Hollywood jumped with vigour on the martial arts bandwagon.

The popularity of martial arts cinema that kicked off in the mid-1940s changed the texture of fight scenes on the screen. These films gave fans what most excited them: ferocious battles between skilled martial artists. Judo, karate and other disciplines began to change the way audiences conceptualized and experienced hand-to-hand combat.

One of the most multitalented martial arts enthusiasts of twentieth-century Hollywood was Bruce Tegner, whose career spanned more than fifty years as a practitioner of disciplines from judo to karate, along with several other of the fighting arts. Tegner's parents, who were judo and jujitsu instructors, took pains to ensure their son got his start training in martial arts at the age of two. Tegner was also a prolific writer, the author of nearly a dozen books on karate, judo and related subjects, and choreographed a fight scene in the 1962 Korean War thriller *The Manchurian Candidate*, which featured Frank Sinatra and Laurence Harvey in starring roles. In 1963 Tegner's devotion to martial arts encouraged him to integrate his expertise in five different schools to create a style of self-defence that he called jukado, based mainly on judo, karate and aikido, with the addition of stick fighting techniques. His published works were instrumental in attracting a number of people from the entertainment world to martial arts. Such was the case of screenwriter and producer Paul Weitz and his younger brother Chris, a film-maker and actor of note.

The 1970s saw David Carradine ascend to prominence with U.S. television audiences as the hero of the TV series *Kung Fu*, in which the Hollywood-born actor played the part of an endearing Shaolin Temple monk on a voyage through the American Wild West. The character he portrayed in this series inspired Carradine to take up kung fu in earnest, which he did as a disciple of the Chinese-American expert Kam Kuen. In recognition of his services to martial arts, in 2015 Carradine was posthumously inducted into the Martial Arts History Museum Hall of Fame.

Seventh Dan aikido master Steven Seagal also stands out as one of the most controversial screen stars to boast a proficiency in martial arts. 'Tall and lean, with the rough, good looks of a daredevil jet pilot, Steven Seagal is more than just a martial-arts wizard who can flip a man five feet in the air with a flick of his wrist,' as reported in a *Los Angeles Times* biographical feature.

> A decade ago [1978], he was living in Japan, where he taught Aikido and, by his own account, was recruited by the CIA to help carry out undercover missions. A year ago, he returned to the States and was quietly running his West Hollywood-based Aikido Ten Shin Dojo, a martial-arts school, where he still teaches three nights a week.[18]

Seagal launched his cinematic career in 1988 with *Above the Law*, which marked the first time aikido was featured on screen in a combat scene. This debut swiftly launched him to a prominent place on the list of the leading tough-guy contemporaries of his day. The most outstanding names in this category include: Arnold Schwarzenegger, who trained in karate and was awarded an honorary black belt in taekwon-do; Clint Eastwood, who is now is a practitioner of jujitsu; Sylvester Stallone, who holds a black belt in karate, and appeared in several films, most notably *Rocky* and *Rambo*, in which he played the role of a hard-bitten bruiser in possession of deadly martial arts skills; and the late Chuck Norris, another star who brought to the screen his fighting abilities in judo, Brazilian jiujitsu and the Korean mixed martial art of Tang Soo Do.

Seagal has since sparked animosity among some of his enthusiasts, as well as the population at large. He identifies as a Republican hardliner and in 2014 he suggested that Barack Obama should be impeached for the tragedy of Benghazi, when a U.S. ambassador and three other Americans were killed in the Libyan city. Two years later, in 2016, it came to light that Vladimir Putin had awarded Russian citizenship to the Hollywood star and fellow martial artist.

The pair have attended combat sessions together and Seagal has more than once lavished praise on Putin as a great world leader. The American actor went so far as to support the 2014 Russian annexation of Ukraine's Crimea. In a 2023 interview, Seagal declared, 'I am one million per cent Russophile and one million per cent Russian,' and to emphasize his point, the American actor now resides in Russia.[19]

A drum roll would make an appropriate introduction to the biggest name in show business to have excelled in martial arts. Elvis Presley exploded onto the Hollywood screen in the 1956 musical *Love Me Tender*. From that day onwards, the crooner began rocketing to what seemed the heights of stardom. The screeching brake on his career came a year after the film's release. On 20 December 1957, Presley received an unexpected and, truth be told, unwanted Christmas gift from Uncle Sam: it was a letter ordering him to report to his local recruitment station to be conscripted into the U.S. Army. Millions of fans wept bitter tears over the loss of their singer hero and the army barber's pruning of his illustrious mound of hair.

Elvis was stationed with U.S. troops in Germany, where he came into contact with Jürgen Seydel, a martial artist acknowledged by his admirers as the father of karate in Germany, in those days an almost unknown discipline in the country. Seydel sparked Elvis's interest in the Japanese style of combat that was to become a lifelong activity, at least in the fewer than twenty years he had left to live. Indeed, Elvis contributed greatly to the popularization of karate in the United States after his return from active duty in 1960. When off on annual leave, Elvis headed to Paris to train under the Japanese Shotokan karate master Tetsuji Murakami. Elvis was so determined to perfect his karate that on one of these trips he spent nine days working ceaselessly in Murakami's dojang, breaking boards with his knuckles and strengthening his kicks and punches.

Elvis incorporated karate into his later life activities, particularly in the 1974 film *The New Gladiators*, inspired by Ed Parker, a karate master who trained Elvis, along with other cinema celebrities and stunt men. It was Parker who tutored Elvis up to his 1st Dan black belt, being awarded an honorary 8th Dan in 1974. The documentary was financed by Elvis and chronicles the official U.S. karate team's partaking in the 1973 European championship matches. The film was never shown and vanished after Elvis's death in 1977, only to be discovered in 2001 in the back of a lorry in a Hollywood garage. After several months of restoration work, it was released a year later, incorporating footage of Elvis practising karate. After his death, Elvis's dedication to karate found its reward with a place in the Martial Arts History Museum Hall of Fame in California, alongside martial arts legends Bruce Lee and Jackie Chan.

5

AWAKENING THE SPIRIT

You must be like water in order to achieve a high level of spirituality in martial arts. Fluidity in movement and agility of thought are the prerequisites needed to instil in the practitioner power, success and a meaningful existence. This was the message bequeathed by Bruce Lee, whose fighting movements flowed with a liquid flexibility that rendered the kung fu master at one with his surroundings. Empty your mind, be formless, shapeless – like water.

Taekwon-do, aikido and judo are a few of the traditional martial arts, mostly of Japanese origin, that incorporate the suffix *do* in their names. This signifies the vocalization of the Japanese *kanji*, which can be translated as 'way' or 'path'. These disciplines are collectively acknowledged to represent a road paved with arduous physical training, one that eventually leads the dedicated follower to a life of spiritual peace and fulfilment.

'Much of the mystical power surrounding the martial arts and its superhuman deeds stems from the Eastern concept of *chi* or *qi*,' explains martial arts historian John Corcoran.

> *Chi* is the biophysical energy, or life force, or internal power possessed by every person. It can be generated through a combination of sustained concentration and abdominal breathing

> techniques . . . Ideally, *chi* can infuse a person with tremendous vitality and, when manifested physically, can make him or her extremely powerful in action, much more so than the power developed purely through the muscular system alone.[1]

'Chi is a life force that runs through every living being,' says taekwon-do instructor Keiron Henderson. 'In martial arts, it is relevant to the point that our strikes and defences are focused on chi, making our actions purposeful and meaningful. A strike without the use of chi is just a gesture, while using it is to show will with a purpose.'[2]

Water is the most flexible of substances. It adapts seamlessly to its environment, be it a glass, the banks of a river or the shores of the sea. There is no inner struggle, no hesitancy in its actions. Water realizes its fulfilment by synchronizing with its surrounding circumstances. Likewise, in the world of martial arts success will be reached not only through physical prowess, but more crucially by harnessing the mind and focusing on the spiritual and philosophical elements. This is the crucial aspect habitually overlooked by most people who sign up for training in martial arts.

The brutality of fight scenes flaunted to the public in Hollywood films in no way reflects the philosophy of martial arts, none of which advocate gratuitous violence under any circumstances. Take into consideration, for instance, the five tenets of taekwon-do that must be memorized and recited by students in the dojang: courtesy, integrity, perseverance, self-control, indomitable spirit. These are the codes that have been set down to guide the practitioner's character as well as their physical development.

Martial arts in their purest form are much more than a physical contest between two opponents, a means of imposing one's will or inflicting damage upon another person. Too many aspirants take up martial arts simply to acquire fighting skills, often driven by the influence of kung fu films. They do so with the aim of impressing others, or in the mistaken belief that this is a way to build strength of character. What they fail to comprehend is that personal strength lies in a person's ability to reject violence and conflict, to walk away from provocation without any fear of humiliation, confident in the knowledge that there is no need to prove themselves. Expertise in martial arts is not intended to be a mandate for imposing pain and suffering on others. Quite to the contrary, a truly strong practitioner will shun aggressive behaviour, being aware of the damage that can be inflicted on others, as well as the prospect of facing criminal charges for causing grievous bodily harm. A martial artist has no need to embrace violence. It was the sixth-century BCE Chinese general and philosopher Sun Tzu who said, 'To fight and conquer in all your battles is not supreme excellence: supreme excellence consists in breaking the enemy's resistance without fighting. To win one hundred victories in one hundred battles is not the highest skill. To subdue the enemy without fighting is the highest skill.'[3]

'To understand martial arts properly, it is necessary to take account of the psychological and metaphysical as well as the technical aspects,' explains author Peter Payne. 'Above all, it is vital to understand how a physical activity, seemingly loosely related to the fields of pure sport such as prize-fighting or wrestling, can come to deal with such matters as psychospiritual transformation and the nature of reality.'[4]

The name of Bodhidharma has been cited several times as the Indian monk who, on his travels across Asia some two millennia ago, was said to have spent more than nine years living in a cave near the Shaolin Monastery in China. After almost a decade of solitude, Bodhidharma's days and nights of deep contemplation gave birth to the art of kung fu, a technique he crafted for the monks so they could defend themselves against marauders and other evildoers. Legend or historical truth, the fact is that Bodhidharma today stands as the patriarch of tens of millions of kung fu students around the world. What this tale brings to light is that the martial art he created in Asia was founded on the back of years of deep-rooted spiritual reflexion.

Centuries later, in the sixteenth century, martial arts began to integrate the concept of spiritual growth, coinciding in time with more peaceful days in Asia, mainly China and Japan. Once the domain of mortal combat between armies and individual enemies, martial arts came to represent a route of spirituality, one that enriched the participant's personal life. Swordsmanship was transformed into the philosophical *Kendo*, or 'the way of the sword' instead of the art of fighting with a bladed weapon. The pacific expression *do*, meaning 'the way', was attached to the traditional martial arts, such as taekwon-do, aikido and judo.

'Martial arts have a competitive nature,' says Norli García, a contributor to the broadcasting network *Whistlekick*.

> But if we are able to harness the spiritual side of it, it can take us into a meaningful journey of self-realisation, which then leads to self-discovery and self-improvement. Rejecting the spiritual side of martial arts will only wreak havoc because you are ignoring the thermostat that sets the temperature of such a powerful weapon. It is the self-control to not engage in physical battle or avoid it altogether, even though you know very well that you have the upper hand against your challenger.[5]

There is a samurai proverb that states, 'The angry man will defeat himself in battle as well as in life.' The message is clear: victory lies in the warrior's ability to exercise self-control. The samurai must at all costs avoid the exhausting struggle of suppressing one's emotions, otherwise it will only bring the inverse of what can be realized through calm reflexion. Author Joe Hyams stresses this point in his exploration of Zen and its role in the practice of martial arts.

The name Zen refers to a Buddhist school of beliefs that became particularly prevalent in Japan in the fourteenth century. Historically, it is deemed to be the fulfilment of ancient traditions of Indian and Chinese culture that rooted itself most deeply in the spiritual values of Japan. Zen originated in India as the Dhyana school, founded by the much-cited and semi-legendary Bodhidharma, who introduced it into China, where it became known as the Chan school. Zen differed from most schools of Buddhism in disregarding the canonical texts and instead emphasizing that only by self-knowledge and introspection could truth be attained. At a certain point the effect of such discipline would come in the form of a sudden intuition of the ineffable principles underlying the Universe. In accordance with this doctrine, the monasteries of Zen monks offered no didactic instruction, but by riddles and even a measure of derision they sought to awaken a questing attitude in their disciples. Zen, with its eschewing of metaphysical subtleties and its arduous discipline, gained great support from the dominant military class in Japan, that is, the samurai warriors.

Hyams tells of a meeting one summer day in 1964 with a martial artist that he hoped to persuade to become his instructor. That person was Bruce Lee. Hyams was at first dismayed by Lee's criticism of the martial arts skills he was asked to demonstrate. After explaining to the author that he would have to unlearn all the techniques he had acquired under previous masters, Lee agreed to take him on as a student. Lee then relates the story of an encounter between a university professor and a Japanese master he visited, hoping to be enlightened on the teachings of Zen.

> The master listened patiently and finally suggested they have tea. The master poured his visitor's cup full and then kept on pouring. The professor watched the cup overflowing until he could no longer restrain himself. 'The cup is overfull, no more will go in.' 'Like this cup,' the master said, 'you are full of our own opinions and speculations. How can I show you Zen unless you first empty your cup?'

Bruce then asked Hyams if he had understood the point.

'Yes,' I said, 'you want me to empty my mind of past knowledge and old habits, so that I will be open to new learning.'

'Precisely,' Lee replied.[6]

Clearing the mind is a task inherent in the teachings of Sun Tzu and other Eastern philosophers. It is laid down as a goal of supreme importance for any martial artist. The ultimate aspiration is to attain a state of *mu*, a Japanese phrase signifying 'marvellous new power' in an individual. The ancient sages who taught martial arts placed great emphasis on the need to keep one's eye open to introspection and the liberation of the mind. Karate Grandmaster Kazumi Tabata advanced the hypothesis of *tanren* (discipline or training), which is the effort to burn out the energy of one's mind and body with symbolic burning flames. This requires reaching the deepest roots of mental integration and concentration.

Tabata based his teachings on *tanren* as a means to acquiring a durable mind, which in turn fosters an exquisite ability to withstand pain and distractions. Once the practitioner acquires this state of mind, a person's external consciousness and unconscious form a connection. 'When they connect, one acquires spiritual power and an ability to cope with things naturally,' he says. 'Fear is something one has to get over through *tanren*. To get over it, one needs to train one's observation on the mind and develop the strength of will. When one becomes conscious by sensing the function of the mind and the truth of the Universe, one's fear disappears.'[7]

Bruce Lee, Joe Hyams and other notables speak of the key role played by spirituality in martial arts, a perception that is ingrained in all the major traditional schools. Judo, widely accepted to be one of the oldest formal martial arts, as well as karate, taekwon-do and most of the others, hold to the idea that a meditative state of mind is a prerequisite for mastery of their respective arts. The message is clear: the mind must remain calm, fully open and free of distortion or anxiety. There can be no thought of self, no emotion, no sense of fear. Mind and body, inner and outer, need to act in complete harmony.

SOME YEARS AGO, a martial arts master by the name of Cole travelled to the Philippines to pay a visit to his friend Frank. When they met in Manila, Cole learnt that Frank was under threat from a villainous millionaire, Charles Venarius, who was plotting to lay his hands on Frank's land, which contained valuable oil deposits. Cole stepped in, making use of his martial arts skills to defend his friend. In retaliation, Venarius hired a ninja, Hasegawa, to murder Frank. Cole, who was himself schooled in the ninja fighting art of ninjutsu, defeated and killed Hasegawa, having already disposed of Venarius with the classic ninja weapon, a bladed *shuriken*. This is the plot of Menahem Golan's 1981 martial arts film *Enter the Ninja*, with the Italian actor Franco Nero in the starring role.

The film was a mega-hit and denoted a milestone in what was emerging as a national craze for this newly discovered spectacular fighting form. Two years after the release of *Enter the Ninja*, the Sam Firstenberg-directed thriller *Revenge of the Ninja* hit the screens, starring the Japanese multi-martial arts expert Sho Kosugi, with his son Kane Takeshi Kosugi in the supporting role as the victim of a brutal mob of gangsters. Riding this cinematographic high, in 1984 Israeli-American film director Firstenberg rewarded his voracious audiences with *Ninja III: The Domination*, the third in his Ninja trilogy, with Sho Kosugi once again starring.

The world of fictional entertainment was quick to jump on the ninja bandwagon that had taken martial arts fans by storm in the 1980s. The prime exponent of this trend was *Teenage Mutant Ninja Turtles*, which began life as a comic series created in 1984 by graphic artists Kevin Eastman and Peter Laird. The story follows the adventures and misadventures of four humanlike turtles skilled as ninja warriors, who set out to fight crime in New York City.

'The image of the Ninja as a black-clad, mysterious, super-samurai who is a deadly assassin and spy is the popular concept [that] the word brings to mind today,' relates martial arts historian Stephen Turnbull. 'All these elements have some basis in reality.'[8] The ninja's traditional values encompass the defence of certain principles on the battlefield and the unalterable dignity of warrior-class ethics. These values invoked the reflection of a warrior with deadly expertise in combat techniques.

Guerrilla warfare, assassination, espionage, magic and mysticism comprise the lifeblood of this shadowy individual. All well and good, but can the ninja truly be considered a member of the martial arts community? What constitutes a martial art, in its simplest form, has been previously defined as a fighting art created for combat between two or more opponents. It is the deployment of military tactics with artistic skill. On the basis of this definition, the way of the ninja ticks all the boxes.

'One might say that if the 1970s was the decade of kung fu, karate and samurai, the 1980s gave us Shaolin monks and Ninjas,' notes author Paul Bowman. Indeed, 1980 saw the popular novel *Shōgun* – featuring ninjas as terrible assassins – televised in a series starring Richard Chamberlain. In the same year, Chuck Norris's ninja-focused film *The Octagon* was premiered, also depicting ninjas as villains. 'But perhaps more importantly,' says Bowman, 'was the release of *American Ninja*. This was a huge success, which spawned multiple sequels spanning the rest of the 1980s into the 1990s.'[9]

The unique martial arts skills of the secretive fighters of ancient Japan have for decades held the curiosity of martial arts fans across the world. But who were (or are) these mystic warriors? Ninjutsu brings into play a system of subtle strategy, stealth, psychological manoeuvring and tactics rooted in evasion. Direct confrontation is to be avoided whenever possible. Instead, the ninja deploys an expertise in exploiting an opponent's force to achieve victory with a minimum expenditure of effort. Stealth and deception are the primary psychological tools in the ninja's arsenal.

The ninja symbol is the Japanese character *nin*, which translates as endurance and strength. These warriors traditionally held sway in Japan's mountains, where they aroused great respect and fear in their potential or real enemies. Ninja history, some verging on the romantic, abounds with tales of black-clad, secretive warriors stalking their prey beneath the moonlight, before disappearing in an imaginary puff of smoke.

Kung fu instructor and television presenter Chris Crudelli spent time in Japan's Chiba Prefecture training camp, an experience he says offered a fascinating glimpse into the life of the modern-day ninja. 'The ninja master, often assisted by his most experienced students, not only teaches ninjutsu fighting skills, but is also an expert in the philosophies, tactics and lifestyle of the ancient night warriors,' he explains.[10]

In previous chapters it has been shown how the practice of martial arts can have a profound and positive impact on people's lives. Melanie D. Gibson found in taekwon-do her salvation from a self-destructive existence, while Chionia Christodoulelli Myrsini emphasizes that Shaolin kung fu and tai chi have contributed to her overall health and well-being. Rena Glickman found in judo an escape from gang violence on the streets of Brooklyn. Bruce Lee turned his back on Hong Kong street brawls and conflict with the police to devote his short life to the practice of Jeet Kune Do. Josiah Farrelly found in Muay Thai a way of building his self-confidence, making it a major influence in his daily life.

What about the practice of ninjutsu? Can a cultural outsider penetrate the enigmas of this guarded society? Christopher Springham, a consultant in sustainability, travelled to Japan to find out.

> I was 57 years old and burned out from my job, working long hours with too much flying. I loved my work and colleagues. We built a world-leading renewable energy company, but at some point my own energy began to peter out. After enduring the sustained misery of our business being acquired by a blue-chip American corporation, I banked my cheque and lazily typed into Google, 'Get me out of here!'
>
> I spotted a rough web link, partly in English, partly Japanese. 'Train as a Ninja. Musashi Clan, Tokyo.' I found the Musashi Clan online and checked it out. I signed in to a

sketchy-looking portal, paid them €800 and booked a flight to Japan.

The dojo hides beneath a grey 1970s office block. I found a small, ordinary door in the back marked 'Musashi Clan' and entered a dim, concrete corridor. Slowly, others arrived. Most were young men, mid-twenties, strong, lithe and from their movements they were clearly martial arts practitioners. One was from China, the other twelve were from Korea including a single girl. We removed our shoes, entered the dojo, sat cross-legged in a circle and did not speak. Eventually, two slender men in floor-length black robes joined us. They arrived from behind a curtain and said nothing. Everyone sat watching as they issued a pair of *geta* (wooden slippers), some *jimbe* (thin black pyjamas) and a brown envelope. I opened mine. It contained two rail tickets and a label with my name on it.

We embarked on a four-day journey involving three trains and a small ferry. We travelled to Sendai and onwards to Sakata in Yamagata Prefecture, where we disembarked and travelled by bus to a small, dilapidated *hosuteru* (hostel) on the edge of an open natural park. There was no briefing or explanation of what was to come. The following days were marked by a giant 'wide game' in the open air without any sense of what was to happen or whether there was a puzzle to solve. The exercises, I now realize, were to isolate the strategic clarity of thought necessary to qualify in the samurai arts by the brutal application of lessons learned in the dojo. This was achieved by applying the ninja skills we had learned through real and subjectively often terrifying, experiences. The prize, we were told, was that anyone who could reach the *kokorozashi* or goal might be considered a samurai 'novice'. I learned from this that goals are at once metaphysical and physical.

In fact, I was separated from the group, heavily blindfolded, bound by the ankles and wrists with my hands behind my back, driven some distance and dumped on hard ground. It was late morning and I remained there all afternoon until evening approached. I could still feel the sun on my body. I was kicked in the small of the back and heard footsteps of my captors departing before the vehicle disappeared. Quite quickly I became very scared and worn out. It began to get cold. I cried out. What the hell was I thinking by putting myself in this situation? It extended for many hours and lasted well into the night.

There is a moment, I can't draw now exactly when because I had no grasp of real time, when you 'lose' your ego. You are done. Your anger cedes. Despair creeps in. The fear remains but a certain resignation evolves. All that mattered was the cold and the fear. I have no idea how long I lay there, it was several hours. Suddenly in the distance I could hear a vehicle approaching. I was lifted up and placed in the back of a van. There were two men holding me, controlling the situation. I couldn't see them but I could feel their grip.

I didn't know anything except the fact it was night-time and I had been outdoors in the middle of nowhere. My captors were also eating. It seemed an oddly civilized interlude given my plight. I began speaking in English, requesting my release and asking for help. No answers. The doors were closed and I sat with my back to the side of the van as we slowly drove over bumpy ground and then stopped. I presumed we were at a camp and there would be some respite.

Worse was to come. They retied my ankles. They then retied my wrists but this time there was a loud crash and my arms jerked upwards behind me. I was standing but somehow attached to a rope. I could not quite touch the ground fully. I was on tiptoes, and with my hands pulled upwards behind me it felt like my shoulders were going to dislocate. I could move backwards and forwards as though on a rudimentary pulley. But I couldn't free myself. I yelled and screamed and protested but was blindfolded, cold and bound.

I listened as the van disappeared. As time passed I was somehow claimed by a cold reason and an ounce of resignation. This might be where courage lies. There is some unutilized resource inside us when we become prey. As my anger and ego left me, a sense of enquiry began to occupy my head. I shuffled backwards and boom, I collided with the trunk of a tree. I remember leaning against it and working my way further around it. It's hard to tiptoe on a root in wooden shoes. By wiggling to find larger stones to put my feet on, I was able to eventually lift the rope along the branch; as I jiggled to do this, I realized the bark edges would fray the rope and it did so, especially when I applied and relieved the pressure with my body weight. When one loop of the rope was almost severed, it was possible to loosen the knot and finally my hands were free.

I had been able to feel that to my left on the ground was a metal object. I hadn't been able to feel the material through my wooden soles. I imagined it was a root. But when I then picked it up, I recognized it. A *kunai*. It's a short metal hand tool with a looped handle and a fairly sharp blade. It can be used for cutting and also for climbing. You can stab it into a trunk or between stones to make a foothold. On a piece of cord it can also be thrown a short distance and then retrieved. Along with various *shuriken* (sharpened throwing stars) and *nunchaku* (a chained club widely used in various martial arts) it is a common part of the ninja arsenal. I made observations. Oddly my blindfold had conditioned me to 'operate' in darkness. I noticed I was using feel more than sight to execute the task of releasing myself. I felt changed. I wasn't scared. I felt tired and cold and sore but actually strong – strong inside anyway. Using the *kunai* to free my feet, I stood up slowly and breathed, then I gathered the rope and started stumbling my way in wooden shoes back to the hostel.

When I woke it was mid-morning and the sunlight was bright through the door onto the floor. Of the nine on the train, seven remained, including the girl, and of those in the room, two were injured. One had a nasty gash on his leg, which I saw when it was dressed, and the other was moaning like a baby. We sat in the quiet and awaited the next turn of events. I sat next to the girl. She showed me her ID and I showed her my passport. She was 22, born in Seoul. She was showing me now a core ninja principle that what cannot be achieved alone can be managed by more than one person with effective communication and a plan.

When night fell we were blindfolded, wrists bound once again and driven in the van. Periodically the vehicle stopped, doors were opened and someone was ushered out. I think I was last, I don't know. No objective was described or expressed but it was natural to presume we should try to return to base. I removed my blindfold and inspected it properly for once. I found a road, it led over a hill to my right and weirdly there was a bus stop. I headed back into the woods and heard a noise

Musashi master subjects Christopher Springham
to sword training without sympathy.

to my right. Someone was calling out. They were obviously captured by assailants in the woods. I decided to head in the opposite direction. By running in short bursts I found I could move quickly and then stop to listen.

To my left I started to hear sounds of a pursuit. After the experience of the first two days, I felt no trust whatsoever in the guides. I was well aware of their capabilities; they were very rough and showed no warmth towards anyone. I was unsure they were acting in anyone's interest except to orchestrate a cruel game for their own entertainment. I realized I was behaving like prey and leaving a trail of noise and tracks. I'd dashed intermittently for several miles. I stopped, breathed and listened to myself. The natural behaviour in flight is to dash and escape. The opposite behaviour works far more effectively. I remembered the knots on my wrists, the place after the fear, the calm clarity of it.

The pursuit I heard had ended in capture because the voice of the victim was audible and there was rustling inconsistent with the regular sound of the wood. I knew at least two were down, but I didn't know where I was heading until way ahead of me someone lit a flare. As I progressed, the flare was perhaps 40 metres [130 ft] in front of me when I heard a loud thump and some protests. The voice of the girl and one of the young men. I couldn't understand what they were saying (had I been a true ninja I am sure this would have been possible) but they had clearly walked into a trap. I crept step by step toward the gap in the trees where I could clearly identify two figures bound to saplings about 10 metres [33 ft] apart. I was utterly convinced they had been abandoned. They were whispering to each other in Korean but not distressed.

I quietly appeared from a distance of perhaps 10 metres away, then came to the girl first, pushed my *kunai* into her hand and moved on to the man. I was perhaps only a metre away from him when I hit the ground. I really went down hard. I had been grabbed by a guide right next to me and didn't even see him. He had been lying on the ground beneath his robe. This trainee had made a miserable mistake. The captives were bait. In my distorted chronology and the reaches of time, it seemed many hours until I was approached by a figure who began to work at the knots by my wrists with the bladed tool. It was the girl. She had concealed my *kunai*, cut her own bonds and approached to cut mine. She cut the rope from my wrists, handed the *kunai* to me and fled, softly and swiftly into the woodland.

I walked towards the sun as it rose, treading softly. I let out a childish yelp when a hand grasped my shoulder. A guide was right behind me. He must have been following me the whole time. I had done everything possible to avoid detection and yet I was caught like a child in a playground. He nodded towards a tree opposite where a *shuriken* star was embedded. It showed a path home.

When I reached the hostel, no one else seemed to be around. The door was open and unoccupied. No one returned for hours. Around midday a guide returned and saw me waiting outside the hostel. Taking the van he headed off towards the road I had found, covering perhaps a mile of track before reaching the road with a plume of dust behind him and a crackle of loose stones beneath the tyres.

With a bad back, a sore knee and stinging toes I made it into the hostel, checked out my little case and found my phone. It was dead and there was no sign of the charger. Not much use. I hurriedly concealed my gear and romped back to the front porch with a cup of hot water and a rice cake and continued waiting. Eventually the van returned with three other men, the girl, two guides and a new, much taller, figure I recognized from the dojo. He wore a full black robe. He also carried a wooden long sword and had a short wooden sword at the waist. It was the samurai. He didn't say much but he did show us a map of the island. It indicated the track to the road, the route of the road to a small settlement beyond the hill, the widespread woodland, a river, with a lake nearby, a huge hill at the head of a valley and a temple. Then he placed his hand on the *katana* – his wooden long sword, indicating the soul of the warrior. I resolved to get the hell out of there by any means possible – but not without winning the contest and graduating as a samurai novice. I wanted to hold that sword.

When I woke it was dark again. I realized immediately what had happened. They [the other novices] had all made an early dash in the hope of reaching the temple first. With the ninja and particularly a samurai in pursuit, I didn't fancy their chances. I sat on the front porch as the stars grew brighter and contemplated slipping into my *jimbe* and *geta* once more before heading to the woodland and round the lake, over the hill and down to the temple gate. Each time we had learned something in the dojo we had been shown how to adapt it. Adapt a method. Make it work to deliver the outcome whatever the circumstances. Look for the sharp edges and a tool will come to hand. Wait, watch, listen, let time be your friend. Put patience before action despite the pain. Be calm. Set ego aside. Seek clarity.

Eventually an elderly gentleman in a battered car approached quite slowly. I flagged him down and pointed up the hill. I was clearly from elsewhere but he seemed unperturbed as we set off. He pointed at the *fukiya* I had [a Japanese blowgun] and made a joke gesture with his fist like the girl had shown me. A junction approached and he dropped me off by another bus stop. We reached the centre of the village on the hillside. I walked straight into a bar. There has been much written about the curative and inspirational qualities of beer but never in my life has anything tasted so wonderful. The tourist brochure in the bar pointed to the exact location of the temple and the downhill path towards it. As I looked through the front window of the bar, there was a minibus filled with American tourists fussing with bags and macs and water bottles and cameras. I stepped out behind Chuck from Chattanooga and Mandy from Minnesota on their promenade to the candlelit temple in the valley. The whole while I was wondering if we would reach the temple gate directly ensuring I wasn't noticed – my use of ninja deflection perfectly executed – and how the defence of the gate would be managed by the guides.

I've always applied 'Banzai Logic', a concept I had read about in ninja comics, where action without hesitation in a desperate situation is better and more likely to end in glory than hesitation. Here I was, 180 metres [590 ft] from the gate, bold as brass and bound for glory. I still had the *fukiya* in my hand, and I could barely drop it before a figure in black came by the gate: the samurai. Ten metres away. I suddenly felt an iron grip on my wrist, burning as it twisted and my arm was whipped back with such force I had to turn away. It was the guide. To our right from across the road came a slender, nimble figure running at full tilt for the gate. It was the girl. She had obviously been waiting there, evading capture and remaining patient. The guide hesitated for just a moment, his iron grip loosened and I tore away.

I was consumed with pride for having made it, oldest by miles, the least combative but one of the two best listeners. The girl fell and I helped her up, and we approached the samurai inside the gate. We touched the hilt of the samurai's wooden longsword and received a bow. I was overwhelmed with pride.

> I flew home after a brief rest day in Tokyo. It took me about six months to recover physically. I went on to use samurai thinking at the close of my corporate career, as a leader in sustainable business, and still do. I remain in awe of Banzai Logic.[11]

From the foregoing, there can be little doubt that ninjutsu is secretive, brutal and can even be lethal. But is there a spiritual element lurking beneath the surface in this age-old sect? Indeed there is, says Yuji Yamada, a lecturer in the Department of Humanities at Japan's Mie University. Yamada explains that during Sengoku period from the fifteenth to the seventeenth century, ninjas may have infiltrated enemy castles, ambushed enemies, committed acts of arson and so on, but their most important job was to deliver information about the enemy to their masters. In order to complete such missions, they actually needed to avoid combat as much as possible, in order to survive and return alive. Even during peacetime, they had roles such as finding out the circumstance of other countries and delivering information to be used for better governance.

During the Edo period of the seventeenth to nineteenth century, when the necessity of combat had become rare and Japanese society was at peace, a ninja's professional function was focused more on information gathering. 'Additionally, a Ninja's spirituality was emphasized,' says Yamada,

> the concept of enduring everything by restraining oneself and prioritising loyalty to one's master was clarified and perseverance began to have more significance. Various martial arts were born during the Edo period and they all emphasised the spiritual aspect. The reason for this might be because there

was very little actual combat, the Shogunate government control during the Edo period was stable, and Confucian moral principles permeated. Furthermore, unless spirituality was emphasised, Ninjutsu could have been abused.

Yamada affirms that ninjas do not loudly reveal their presence or achievements but rather focus on executing their mission for their master quietly and with a high level of spirituality. The inner life of ninjas has been kept under a veil, albeit releasing to the surface many elements of their lives to stir our imagination. Because of that, there have been numerous images of the ninja, created in

Women students demonstrating martial arts,
Yenching University, Beijing, China, 1928.

different time periods as well as by different ethnic groups. 'But fundamentally,' he explains, 'because the presence of Ninjas matched the values of Japanese people, they have been accepted in Japan as well as throughout the world to this day.'[12]

The spiritual enlightenment that can be achieved through the practice of martial arts began to gain a degree of magnetism among mainly young people predominantly in the later 1960s through to the end of the 1970s, a time we now call the New Age. What might be termed a rejection of Western values arose from events that often triggered protests – and not always peaceful ones – such as the anti-Vietnam War protests of the early 1960s in the United States, the student riots in France in 1968 and the campaign for nuclear disarmament that brought campaigners into the streets throughout most of the Cold War. Significant numbers of dissenters began exploring practices and lifestyles that reflected their rejection of the materialistic, self-centred values of the established order. In this context, the spiritual orientation of Asian martial arts proved highly attractive as a way of achieving a deeper understanding of the inner spirit.

Dutch philosopher Wouter Hanegraaff maintains that this New Age movement has a countercultural logic that focuses on an individualized and/or privatized spirituality. This in turn is centred on a search for a deeper understanding of the self. 'This "de-traditionalisation" of the self,' he says, 'initially combined the rise of the New Age movement and countercultural spiritualities throughout the 1960s and 1970s and converged on the idea of the individual as a self-directing, authorial agent, relying on his or her own sources of authority.'[13]

Asian martial arts have developed over the centuries, in times of peace and war, under the influence of philosophies and religions like Zen Buddhism and Taoism. They have been adopted by the New Age movement, since a number of the goals for practising martial arts are closely aligned with this social and spiritual crusade and provide adherents with a cultural template of practices. The idea of cultivating the harmonized body–mind relationship through martial arts forms is typical of Zen- and Taoist-inspired arts and strongly compatible with principles that see every human as a unique, holistic relationship of body, mind, emotions and spirit. Expressed in Zen terms, it may be asserted that by grasping and absorbing the spiritual elements in martial arts, you become what you were not before.

6

FORWARD MOVES

It is the morning of Monday, 28 April 2025. You are at Madrid's Barajas Airport, waiting for the departure gate of your flight back to London to be announced. You need to chair a board meeting tomorrow morning, or perhaps your family is expecting you to arrive in time to attend your daughter's fifteenth birthday party. The announcement the departure lounge tannoy abruptly blares out is not the one you were expecting to hear. You are told that your flight, in fact all flights, have been cancelled due to a nationwide power outage. Trains, trams and all public transport systems have ceased to function. Cashpoint machines, phones and broadband have failed. Shops cannot take card payments as main electricity has cut out. There are no taxis available to take you back to your hotel, simply because Madrid's traffic light system has collapsed. Restaurants and bars have been plunged into darkness – so much for any hope of a comforting supper.

How do you react to a fiasco of this magnitude, a disruption of normal life on a scale never experienced until now? To begin with, do you allow yourself to capitulate to this unforeseen set of events? Do you shoulder this as a personal disaster, with all the attendant distress and mental anguish that it involves? Conversely, are you capable of recognizing it as an external matter, a phenomenon totally unconnected to your inner self?

Consider another situation, one in which you are more likely to find yourself: you step out of the house to do the morning shopping and shut the door behind you. With a wrenching twist in your stomach, you suddenly realize that in your hurry to get away you have left your keys and all the rest of your daily accessories on the kitchen table, including your mobile phone and the credit cards in your wallet. Does this bring on a rush of anger and anxiety? If so, try reasoning with yourself: yes, all my paraphernalia sits on the other side of this locked door but here, outside in the street – there is *me*. The ability to disregard, within reason, what we see as setbacks, is more important in today's digital world than at any time in the past.

'For all the good things that today's technology has brought us, we don't seem to be getting happier,' says Luke Archer, founder of conflict management training organization Verbal Aikido.

> Indeed, that very technology may be part of the problem. The screens that fill our lives give us many things. They help us find our way to places. They tell us the news. They give us gossip, jokes, music, videos. They sometimes help us do our work. At other times, they are our work. Even in the gym, we are often isolated, working alone on a treadmill or weights machine. Perhaps even watching yet another screen or cut off from the world by our ear buds.[1]

Charles Harris is chief instructor at the London-based Association of Ki Aikido. He was drawn for many reasons to this martial art, which has since become an integral part of himself, as a meditation, an effective means of self-defence and a way of improving physical and mental balance. He says aikido is a constant challenge that is always pushing him at a constant pace. It is an art that always brings

Above and opposite: Charles Harris, aikido chief instructor at the London-based Association of Ki Aikido Club, in class.

the unexpected but, most of all, for Harris it is a source of enjoyment. Harris draws attention to the fact that humans are physical beings that don't live in a digital world. 'A life locked behind a screen is not a human life,' he says.

> Engagement with the physical world is important. If nothing else, it gives a greater sense of satisfaction when we do it right. We have manipulated a bit of the real world and succeeded. A martial art like aikido brings us face-to-face with this real world. A technique that might look great in theory has to withstand interaction with another human being. This gives us a rare opportunity to make physical contact with others in a safe space. For this reason, it works wonders with people who want to overcome their fears.[2]

Aikido tries to develop certain mental and physical attributes that lie dormant in many people. It accentuates the idea that you cannot have one without the other, the mind and body working in unison. If you are driving home and thinking about cooking supper, you cannot perform one or the other task efficiently. In today's ever more aggressive and fragmented world, there is a spectrum of responses, so that you can deal with an attack in an appropriate way, depending on the level of danger. 'In Aikido,' says Harris, 'the message is that fighting gets you nowhere, whereas connecting and moving with the attacker's own energy will help you defuse an attack, often ensuring that both sides can stay safe from harm.'[3]

Harris emphasizes the importance in all martial arts of being in the present moment and not to be focused on what comes next. In

every aspect of life there are those who look backwards and others who look forward. Both are necessary: those who look to the past are important because they remind us to maintain the principles of the art, while those who look forward maintain the flexibility of the art. Taekwon-do and karate, for instance, are built around striking and blocking techniques. Judo is mainly about grappling. Aikido is a blending art, in which the practitioner goes with the opponent's momentum.

The twentieth-century Spanish philosopher José Ortega y Gasset defined the human condition in his book *Meditations on Quixote* in these words: 'I am myself and my circumstances.'[4] He was half-right in that as an individual being, we exist as ourselves and no one else. The core philosophy embedded in any of the traditional Asian martial arts, however, would contend that our 'circumstances' are, or should be, peripheral to our inner selves.

Verbal Aikido's Archer draws attention to the relentless growth of tension in areas such as politics and social inequality, while in some areas it seems as if street violence and general lawlessness are becoming more commonplace every day. When a conversation becomes heated – and, as he warns, many physical attacks begin verbally – in such an instance Archer urges his students to take a deep breath and repeat these words: *right now, we need to listen to each other. I'll listen first.* Archer says that aikido practitioners become keenly aware of this type of energy shift, a lucid reminder that it is time to put their learning into practice. 'That's all you'll need to say, but there is one more thing you'll need to do for it to work,' he says. 'You must put your own views aside for a moment so that you can truly listen. Develop your reflexes to de-escalate conflict.'[5]

Archer says he is especially proud to be bringing his teachings into schools, where children as young as five are learning to contribute meaningfully to the de-escalation of violence. He says that teaching these principles at an early age not only empowers young minds but lays the foundation for a more empathetic and harmonious society.

UNESCO has carried out studies on the impact of martial arts on the lives of young people, concluding that the major benefits lie in the areas of increased self-esteem and confidence, reduced aggression and greater self-control. Overall, according to the international organization, there is moderate to strong evidence that participation in martial arts makes a positive contribution to a young person's development. The findings show that children and youths with lower socio-economic status (SES) are attracted to 'harder' martial arts, with a stronger focus on efficiency, where efficiency is a focus on the results of head-to-head formal or informal competition, with a focus on winning. Children and youths with higher SES appear more attracted to the softer martial arts where there is a higher focus on mastery of movement patterns and on progress achieved.

Kim Si Hyun, Secretary-General of the International Centre of Martial Arts (ICM) says that as examples of sports practices and intangible cultural heritage, the importance of martial arts for young people cannot be overstated. 'Martial arts can foster intercultural dialogue, ethical sport practices and also act as an empowering tool for youth development,' he emphasizes.

> The ICM was officially established in December 2016 with the clear objective of utilising martial arts as an educational method to teach young people the values and life skills that are needed to build a peaceful and non-violent culture, including respect for oneself and others, self-discipline, fair play, resiliency and respect for cultural diversity.[6]

It is not unusual to find children making up half the number of students in karate, taekwon-do or other martial arts classes. In some cases they would have begun training under parental influence, but many have done so on their own initiative for very specific reasons. Out of the mouths of babes . . .

'I took up taekwon-do to learn to defend myself,' says eleven-year-old Saoirse Grabner, who has been training for more than three years at a dojang in London. 'I was inspired by my mum's stepdad, who is a master in the martial art. I find that it has been very helpful in boosting my self-confidence and it is also a good way to make new friends.'

Saoirse, who holds a yellow belt, says that as she progresses, her aim is to perform better and become more precise in her movements in class. 'I am working to move up in the grades and eventually obtain my black belt,' she says. 'I believe more young people should take up taekwon-do. It is a great way to exercise and boost energy, but importantly it also teaches you how to deal with bullying at school. You learn never to engage in violence unless it is unavoidable and you never have to be scared.'

Saoirse says she enjoys the classes as a fun experience. 'We play games as part of our warm-up and I find this develops sharper hand–eye coordination and the ability to focus on a target,' she says. 'This has made it easier for me to focus on things like my maths exams.'[7]

Asier Cía is an eighteen-year-old student from the northern Spanish city of Pamplona, who began training in karate at the age of four. He is the holder of a 1st Dan black belt and is currently training to grade for his 2nd Dan. Asier has given a good account of himself in sparring and kata competitions.

Saoirse Grabner, an eleven-year-old taekwon-do practitioner, London.

My father signed me up for a karate course. He believed this would help me to acquire the self-discipline and patience that I was lacking. I can honestly say that karate has transformed my life, in the sense that I now feel a greater sense of self-esteem and personal motivation in such things as my school work and life in general. It's important not to be spending my days sprawled on the sofa staring at my mobile.

Asier says his karate training has awakened his mind to focus on what is happening in the present moment. 'This is now more

Karate student Asier Cía executing a high side kick.

crucial than ever before, with the growing number of distractions around us,' he says.

> It is also important to learn to defend yourself, but at the same time understand that violence is to be avoided at all costs. That said, if you are cornered and can't get away, you have the skills to deal with physical aggression.
>
> Karate has introduced me to a lot of people, mostly of my age group and many of whom have become good friends. It is good fun to compete together and maintain a positive opinion of one another, regardless of who wins. This is part of the main message, to have patience and respect for all people.[8]

Harris's preferred technique for confronting violence mirrors the advice given by most professional martial artists. Simply put, it is to not be there. 'Why should I hang around to have a fight?' he says.

> I might lose. I might win but get hurt. Even if all goes well, I could find myself spending six hours in a police station, explaining why I threw this poor guy to the ground, with all his mates swearing that I started it. My aim in self-defence is to get on with my life with the least bother. Ideally, that means not being around when things kick off in the first place.[9]

Violence does not often appear in the form of robberies at knife point or mobile phone theft on mopeds. In the twenty-first century, the evolution of martial arts must address the growing challenge of verbal violence, which is ever-present in social interactions. Verbal Aikido's Archer stresses that developing skills in conflict de-escalation is just as crucial as physical defence, as it empowers individuals to navigate tense conversations with clarity, resilience and mutual respect.

> I see conflict de-escalation becoming increasingly central to modern martial arts practice. As tensions rise in personal, professional, and global contexts, the ability to defuse hostility, engage skilfully in difficult conversations and foster constructive exchanges will only grow in importance. The martial arts of the future will likely integrate emotional intelligence and communication mastery alongside physical technique.[10]

There is a common misapprehension shared by many that visualizes martial artists as young, highly fit athletic males. This false impression fails to take into account the many middle-aged to elderly persons who are regular practitioners and those with physical disabilities who not only participate but excel in their chosen disciplines. Soo Bahk Do (SBD) is a Korean martial art developed by Grandmaster Hwang Kee in the mid-twentieth century, built around principles of karate and kung fu. In 2004 the New York Institute of Technology undertook a study of eighteen men and women to determine the fitness level of martial art practitioners between the ages of forty and sixty. Half of these volunteers were sedentary, while the other half regularly attended SBD classes. They were tested for body composition, balance, flexibility, quadriceps strength, grip strength, muscle endurance and aerobic capacity. The tests identified significant differences between the groups for most of the physical fitness tests.

'The SBD practitioners displayed greater aerobic capacity, balance, flexibility, muscle endurance and strength, and less body fat than the sedentary controls matched for age and sex. SBD can be considered an excellent form of exercise for the promotion of fitness in adults,' according to the report. 'Health professionals should be aware that there are alternative methods to traditional exercise that can increase the physical fitness and health of the middle-aged population.'[11]

There is a quite understandable concern among older people about sustaining an injury while practising a martial art. A ten-year-old will generally bounce back up if slipping or being kicked to the floor. A sixty-year-old is more likely to end up in a hospital emergency ward. This helps explain the fact that a tai chi class is more likely to attract participants above the age of forty than the riskier schools of kung fu, karate and, most of all, taekwon-do. By way of comparison, research shows that compared with karate, the risks of head or neck injury, upper extremity and soft tissue injuries were all higher in aikido. Likewise, the chances of sustaining groin and upper and lower extremity injuries were greater in taekwon-do. There is no evidence of any differences in the number of injuries sustained by men or women.[12]

Having established that kung fu, karate and the other best-known disciplines are by no means the exclusive domain of rugged, sinewy males, the involvement of another sector of society in martial arts training, apart from women and children, merits consideration. The experiences and success stories of the disabled and those with learning difficulties provide a source of deep inspiration.

Paul Abel, who has competed for England, began his lifelong commitment to karate at the age of seven. Within three years he had obtained his 1st Dan black belt, rising to 2nd Dan at sixteen. Abel passed his 3rd Dan grading at age nineteen, rising to 4th when he turned 36. He has since won many karate competitions, including being crowned Commonwealth and British karate champion. He

Woman delivering a karate side kick, showing that the art is accessible to all, including those with disabilities.

also had the honour of being selected as a torchbearer for the London 2012 Olympic Games. He was chosen through the Coca-Cola 'Future Flames' campaign, in its advertising of the Olympics, based on his work in training children and adults with special needs to take part in the martial art.

In 2010 Abel set up a karate school in Surrey, in southeast England. 'After competing at a high level for many years, I wanted to share what I had learnt and give something back to the community,' he says. 'Our instructors really enjoy coaching students, helping them achieve progress in line with their own ambition, pace and capability.'

A year after setting up his club, Abel reflected that it was time to do more with his teaching. While watching TV one day he saw a person with Down's Syndrome, which made him decide to do something for people with disabilities. He visited the Down's Syndrome

Association to explain his wish to work on helping to dispel the widespread assumption that people with disabilities are limited in their activities.

The term 'uniqueness' accurately describes the work Abel and his team are carrying out at the dojang. Students are admitted from the age of three to what Abel defines as an inclusive, community-based undertaking. 'We care about our students and we run classes for all abilities,' he says. 'We are also proud to be the founders and host of the Be Inspired project [a service for people with learning disabilities], encouraging students with disabilities into sport through our term-time classes and school workshops.'

'I persuaded myself that this was not the case and soon after opening my classes to people with all disabilities I found that my efforts had met with great success,' he says.

> Not only can they become proficient in karate, but their training also helps them to achieve physical balance that is important for other activities. Having these students in my classes also teaches children how to communicate and get along with people with disabilities. One of our most precious highlights to date for the Be Inspired project was to have one of our own members, Joseph Clifton, be the first person with Down's Syndrome to be selected for the England Karate Federation's para karate team, which went on to win gold at the 10th Commonwealth Karate Games held in Birmingham in September 2022.[13]

It is difficult enough to envisage a person missing one or more limbs to participate, much less compete, in an activity as physically demanding as judo. Far more astonishing is the prospect of confronting an opponent whose feet and fists are barely visible to martial artists, many of whom have nevertheless walked off with international tournament trophies. Judo has become the most popular martial art for people with visual impairments, those who must rely on their senses and instincts to overcome an opponent. The International Blind Sports Federation (IBSA) World Games are an international multi-sport event that welcomes blind and partially sighted athletes to compete. Their initiative has yielded some truly inspiring results.

Daniel Powell, 28, was born with cone-rod dystrophy, an eye disorder that causes vision loss. It has left him with only 2 per cent of his sight, an impairment that has not deterred him from competing in judo since he was seventeen years old. In 2025 Powell was crowned World Champion at the IBSA World Championships. British team members Kirsten Taylor and Jack Hodgson, also partially-sighted, secured fifth-place finishes.

'I've been in the sport at an elite level for fifteen years on and off, and to finally have a title to my name feels absolutely incredible,' Powell says.

> To actually do it at a World Championships and beat the Paralympic champion means absolutely everything. It's just an incredible feeling, I can't believe it, getting that win right at the end in the final is something I couldn't have really comprehended, but I woke up this morning and just thought stuff it, I'm doing it today. A bit of belief goes a long way.[14]

Physical disabilities do not pose an obstacle in martial arts for anyone with the determination to give it his or her best. Not so long ago, it would have been unthinkable for anyone with a serious physical impairment to consider taking up a life of martial arts. Inclusion is now the catchword for a host of instructors across the range of disciplines.

At the age of ten, Jessica Cox began attending taekwon-do classes at a school in her hometown of Sierra Vista, Arizona. Four years later, she earned her 1st Dan black belt before taking a break from the discipline. While a student at the University of Arizona, Cox restarted her taekwon-do training at an American Taekwondo Association (ATA) club on campus. Nothing remarkable about this martial arts experience, one might be tempted to say. However, it is worth noting that Cox, now 43, was born without arms. In an effort to help future students with this specific disability, her instructors created an entire training curriculum by modifying the standard material from the ATA. For example, instead of a punch, Cox executes a knee strike. Cox has since gone on to earn her third degree taekwon-do black belt and has won the title of Arizona State Champion in forms, or patterns, which in karate are known as katas. Moreover, she chose not to compete in a special abilities ring. In 2019 Cox became a 4th Dan black belt. She has proven her abilities and determination by taking part in other activities, which include surfing, scuba diving and piloting a 1930s American low-wing monoplane called the ERCO Ercoupe.

Karen Roberts, Development Director of the British Judo Association, says that their programme of Adaptive Judo is making recreational and competitive judo accessible for people with disabilities, while empowering them to be part of the community and engage in a physical activity. 'Adaptive Judo accommodates a range of disabilities, from intellectual to physical impairments,' she says. 'It can be integrated into existing projects such as school games festivals. Coaches play a pivotal role in adapting events to meet the needs of participants. Feedback shows that Adaptive Judo not only improves ability and balance but also fosters a sense of belonging among participants.'[15]

Ray Sweeny is a karate 8th Dan who began teaching martial arts at the age of 43. A decade later, he was diagnosed with autism, which did not prevent him from obtaining university degrees in business leadership and psychology.

'Sports weren't something I initially enjoyed,' he says.

> I disliked the aggression and violence in playing, and the bullying attitude of coaches. Paradoxically, I started martial arts at age ten and began practising seriously in my early thirties. My early experiences in martial arts taught me self-discipline and perseverance and over time, I became more confident through the physical skills I had gained. From very early on, I knew I wanted to teach martial arts.

Sweeny was asked by Oxfordshire County Council to teach groups of young people with disabilities: a wheelchair user, an autistic child, one with learning disability, another with compound complex profound disability, children who were blind or deaf or missing limbs. He began to use karate to coach disabled people. 'I did not instruct karate to disabled people – it was the other way around. I used martial arts as a coaching tool,' he says.

Sweeny founded the first disability karate club in the UK, with support from Oxfordshire County Council. One student was a 55-year-old wheelchair user who never looked up and Sweeny was told he had never spoken. 'I talked to him about how we were going to do martial arts and I got really close and then he raised his eyes and looked at me,' he says.

> He didn't move his head at all. I invented something on the spot, forming his hand into a fist and moving his arm to make punches on my palm whilst counting. I stopped at nine and waited. I did this for about three months and one day he said, 'ten'. Soon after he began kicking from his chair. His carers said, 'What have you done? We can't shut him up now'.[16]

Sweeny says he was making connections with people with disabilities whom other coaches could not reach. 'Hundreds of experiences like this have inspired and motivated me even more,' he says. He went on to create participation for 3,000 disabled people in the UK. Receiving an autism diagnosis at age 53 provided a clearer understanding of his lifelong experiences and further strengthened his commitment to creating inclusive environments. He has to date run training sessions for more than 11,000 disadvantaged people, including those from backgrounds of conflict and disaster, physical and sexual violence, NEET (not in education, employment or training), suffering from life-changing disability, PTSD (post-traumatic stress disorder) and physical abuse. 'I believe that martial arts have the potential to foster social cohesion and empower marginalised groups as well as to create sustainable and inclusive opportunities for all,' he says.[17]

Carlos Gutiérrez García is Senior Lecturer at the Department of Physical and Sport Education in Spain's Universidad de León. He maintains that if we agree martial arts can be thought of as systems that blend the physical components of combat with strategy, philosophy, tradition or other features that distinguish them from pure physical reaction, then we will also acknowledge that they will be with us as long as the human species engages in and reflects on combat. 'For many millennia, people have used the power of combat to attack and defend themselves against their enemies, be they real or symbolic, embodiments of fears, desires, deeds, stories, gods or myths,' he says. 'This will continue for thousands of years to come or, at least, until human folly or the whims of fate wipe us off the face of the earth.'[18]

What, then, is the future of martial arts? Or, more accurately, what are the *futures* of martial arts, in this diverse, complex and ever-changing world? Globalization has allowed us to know and engage in martial arts from distant countries, from East to West, from North to South. Some of these practices, such as judo, taekwon-do, MMA or tai chi, can be considered truly global products while others, such as Malaysian Silat, remain for the present time in their infancy. It is likely that more martial arts will reach this global dimension in the coming decades, although access to the highest levels of worldwide recognition seems to be very limited, as evidenced by the Beijing 2008 Olympic Games, where Wushu was not officially included in the Games, or the Paris 2024 Olympics, where karate was excluded, although it was part of the programme for the Tokyo 2020 Games, which took place in 2021 following the COVID-19 lockdowns. Karate's exclusion has sparked some heated discussion and debates within the martial arts community. Several factors contributed to this decision, foremost of which was the Olympic Committee's wish to optimize the Games' appeal to logistical and financial considerations. Karate was dropped primarily due to concerns about what the committee judged to be a lack of universal appeal and its inability to attract a younger audience. Other combat practices, such as MMA, have never been considered, primarily because they lack the historical tradition and aesthetics of more traditional martial arts.

Gutiérrez García says that on an international scale there is a certain desire to return to one's own values and cultural traits. This arises as a reaction to excessive globalization and because of people's longing to recognize and be recognized in their own identity.

> In this context, many martial arts, such as Brazilian Marajoara Wrestling or the old Polish sabre fencing, are being revitalized or recovered from oblivion, to become part of all kinds of cultural and sporting events and even to be integrated into touristic activities. It is foreseeable that this trend will continue in the coming decades, ensuring, to some extent, the preservation of the enormous diversity and cultural richness of martial arts.[19]

One aspect that has been and will continue to be central to the future of martial arts is the question of safety, understood in its broadest sense. Martial arts, with all their practical and scientific evidence and with even greater doses of images and stereotypes created by comic books, TV series, films or YouTube videos continue to gain adherents across the globe. 'These are sold and will continue to be sold as therapies for physical health, mental balance, spiritual peace or the best education for young people,' says Gutiérrez García. He emphasizes that anti-social behaviour is an increasingly prominent feature of our everyday lives:

> Likewise, to face situations of bullying, robbery, sexual aggression, aggression at work or leisure, I fear that in our future society we will have to continue to deal with this reality, in which the 'seeming' is often imposed on the 'being', flooding the practitioner of martial arts with false promises.[20]

In most instances, those who begin training in childhood will remain devoted to their chosen discipline into adulthood or, if not, they will at least retain the psychological benefits of having brought martial arts into their lives. This is important to bear in mind, given that we live in an ever more aggressive world, plagued by uncertainty and hostility. Stories of massacres and political chaos across the globe capture the daily headlines and there is no escaping the threat that these regional conflicts could easily escalate into global warfare. Most of us wish to live in a peaceful and secure environment, so that we can carry out our daily lives with as little anxiety as possible. At the same time, many of us suffer from the lack of self-esteem and spiritual serenity essential to persevere through life in peace and harmony, with ourselves and with those around us. Millions of people across the world have turned to martial arts to achieve this desired state of tranquillity and self-confidence. It is to be hoped that in the future, many more will follow this path to personal fulfilment and well-being.

REFERENCES

1 What Are Martial Arts?

1 Steve Pateman, in conversation with the author, March 2025.
2 Choe Sang-Hun, Jin Yu Young and Victoria Kim, 'South Korea's President Impeached After Martial Law Crisis', *New York Times*, 14 December 2024, p. 25.
3 Carlos Gutiérrez García, *Cuadernos Budo*, vol. II (Barcelona, 2014), p. 13.
4 Keiron Henderson, in conversation with the author, May 2024.
5 Sensei Nicolas Antoine, in conversation with the author, June 2024.
6 John Corcoran, *The Martial Arts Companion* (New York, 1992), p. 40.
7 Greet Angèle De Baets, 'Five Spectrums of Variation in the Narratives of 20 Aikido Experts Worldwide in 2020', *Martial Arts Studies*, 15 (July 2024), pp. 25–37 (p. 25).
8 Ibid.
9 Douglas Wile, 'Taijiquan and Daoism: From Religion to Martial Art and Martial Art to Religion', *Journal of Asian Martial Arts*, XVI/4 (2007), pp. 8–45 (p. 37).
10 Michael Rosenbaum, *The Fighting Arts: Their Evolution from Secret Societies to Modern Times* (Boston, MA, 2002), p. xix.
11 Kim Jae Won, in conversation with the author, April 1983.
12 Peter Lewis, *The Martial Arts* (London, 1996), pp. 69–70.
13 Paul Bowman, *The Invention of Martial Arts* (New York, 2021), p. 32.
14 Mark Li, in conversation with the author, September 2025.
15 Ibid.
16 Jonathan Clements, *A Brief History of the Martial Arts* (London, 2016), p. 135.

17 Bruce A. Haines, *Karate's History and Traditions* [1968] (Rutland, VT, 1997), pp. 12, 14.
18 Clements, *A Brief History of the Martial Arts*, pp. 134–5. The Satsuma clan was prominent for centuries in Japanese history, most notably for leading the revolution against the imperial government in 1877. Satsuma also gave its name to a famous porcelain.
19 Ibid., p. 36.
20 Oscar Ratti and Adele Westbrook, *Secrets of the Samurai* (Rutland, VT, 1973), p. 115.
21 Lewis, *The Martial Arts*, p. 117.
22 Rosenbaum, *The Fighting Arts*, p. 19.
23 Joe Hyams, *Zen in the Martial Arts* (New York, 1979), p. 9.
24 Jiongyan Huang, in conversation with the author, September 2025.
25 Ibid.

2 Whence to Where

1 Rodney Stewart, *Mixed Martial Arts* (Melbourne, 2015), p. 15.
2 Alex Channon, in conversation with the author, July 2025.
3 John Tasker, in conversation with the author, May 2025.
4 Stewart, *Mixed Martial Arts*, p. 41.
5 See Matt Hill's website, www.matthill.co.uk, accessed 2 January 2025.
6 John Tasker, conversation.
7 David Mitchell, *The New Official Martial Arts Handbook* (London, 1984), p. 180.
8 Keiron Henderson, in conversation with the author, September 2024.
9 Josiah Farrelly, in conversation with the author, September 2024.
10 Mitchell, *The New Official Martial Arts Handbook*, p. 182.
11 Statista Research Department, 'Martial Arts Participation in the U.S. 2010–2024', www.statista.com, 26 February 2025.
12 Duk Sung Son and Robert J. Clark, *Korean Karate: The Art of Tae Kwon Do* (Englewood Cliffs, NJ, 1968), p. 5.
13 Donato Nardizzi, in conversation with the author, September 2025.
14 Daniel Beard, in conversation with the author, October 2025.
15 Ibid.
16 Paul Bowman, *The Invention of Martial Arts* (New York, 2021), p. 35.
17 Arthur Conan Doyle, *The Complete Sherlock Holmes* (New York, 1987), pp. 366–7.

18 Bowman, *The Invention of Martial Arts*, p. 51.
19 E. W. Barton-Wright, 'The New Art of Self Defence', *Pearson's Magazine*, March–April 1899, p. 16.
20 Ian Fleming, *Goldfinger* [1959] (London, 2004), p. 124.
21 Quotes from the novelization of Christopher Nolan's (dir.) *The Dark Knight* (2008) by Dennis O'Neil, *The Dark Knight* (London, 2008), pp. 1–2.
22 Ibid., p. 15.

3 Hands Off!

1 AWMA, 'Influential Women in Martial Arts Part 1: Historical Figures', https://blog.awma.com, 8 March 2023.
2 Sensei Gerardo Balves, 'Dojo Notes: Yonamine Chiru, the Most Beautiful and Feared Woman in Okinawa', *Mokuso Magazine*, https://mokuso.ar, 17 October 2022.
3 AWMA, 'Influential Women in Martial Arts'.
4 *London Journal*, June 1722, p. 9.
5 'Ju-Jutsu Suffragettes, a New Terror for the London Police', *Health and Strength*, 6 (1909), p. 42.
6 *Evening Telegraph*, 13 July 1910, p. 6.
7 John Corcoran, *The Martial Arts Companion* (New York, 1992), p. 73.
8 Allie Griffin, '"Hereos" Prevented Monterey Park Shooter from Killing More Victims', *New York Post*, 22 January 2023, p. 16.
9 Cynthia Rothrock, Bill Wallace and Joe Lewis, 'Hard Fight', *Fighter Magazine*, IV/1 (March 1990), p. 47.
10 George Vecsey, 'Judo Champ Doesn't Need Disguises', *New York Times*, 4 November 2016, p. 10.
11 John Garner, 'Karate Reinstatement', *New York Times*, 18 October 1994, p. 15.
12 Alex Vadukul, 'Searching for Lady Kung Fu', *New York Times*, 14 November 1982, p. 12.
13 Alison Fell, 'Taxi Experience', *Spare Rib*, no. 55, June 1977, p. 7.
14 Ibid., pp. 8–10.
15 Rachel Lockton, in conversation with the author, October 2025.
16 Heidi Eggleton and Derek Skea, 'Women's Perceptions of How Martial Arts Influence Their Psychological Well-Being', *Martial Arts Studies*, 16 (December 2024), pp. 8–19.

17 Mark Li, in conversation with the author, October 2025.
18 Myrsini Chionia Christodoulelli, in conversation with the author, October 2025.
19 Master Shi Yan Gui, in conversation with the author, September 2025.
20 Myrsini Chionia Christodoulelli, conversation.
21 Melanie D. Gibson, *Kicking and Screaming: A Memoir of Madness and Martial Arts* (Berkeley, CA, 2021), p. 3.
22 Ibid., p. 31.
23 Ibid., p. 104.
24 Ibid., p. 257.
25 Huang Zhiling and Peng Chao, 'Girl Group Ignites Interest in Kung Fu', *China Daily*, 8 May 2024, p. 34.
26 Ibid.

4 Lights, Camera, Action!

1 Matthew Polly, *Bruce Lee: A Life* (London, 2018), pp. 2–3.
2 Statistics by ABC Glofox: see '13 Martial Arts Industry Trends You Need to Know', www.glofox.com/blog, 19 July 2023.
3 Joe Hyams, *Zen in the Martial Arts* (New York, 1979), p. 9.
4 Donato Nardizzi, in conversation with the author, September 2025.
5 Polly, *Bruce Lee*, p. 430.
6 Davis Miller, *The Tao of Bruce Lee* (London, 2000), p. 97.
7 Polly, *Bruce Lee*, p. 207.
8 Ric Meyers, Karen Palmer and Bill Palmer, *The Encyclopedia of Martial Arts Movies* (Columbia, MD, 1995), p. xiii.
9 Paul Bowman, *Beyond Bruce Lee: Chasing the Dragon through Film, Philosophy, and Popular Culture* (London and New York, 2013), pp. 4–5.
10 Hilda C. Wang, 'Jackie Chan Plots a Conquest', *New York Times*, 16 August 1987, p. 25.
11 Theodore Roosevelt, *An Autobiography* (New York, 1913), pp. 19, 38.
12 Joseph R. Svinth, 'Professor Yamashita Goes to Washington', *Journal of Combative Sport* (October 2000), p. 33.
13 Paul Nurse, 'Pierre Trudeau and Judo', *Gentle Way*, VI/4 (2009), p. 16.
14 Ibid., p. 17.

15 See '5 Presidents Who Studied Martial Arts', https://graciepac.com, 12 September 2018.
16 Al Kamen, 'L.A.'s Lawyer to the Stars – and the Majority Leader', *Washington Post*, 8 February 2007, p. 13.
17 Kirik Jenness, 'Barack Obama, Martial Artist', www.mixedmartialarts.com, 27 July 2016.
18 Patrick Goldstein, 'Steven Seagal Gets a Shot at Stardom', *Los Angeles Times*, 14 February 1988, p. 6.
19 Jacob Stolworthy, 'Steven Seagal Declares Himself "One Million Per Cent" Russian and Lashes Out at U.S. "Disinformation"', *The Independent*, www.independent.co.uk, 16 March 2023.

5 Awakening the Spirit

1 John Corcoran, *The Martial Arts Companion* (New York, 1992), p. 21.
2 Keiron Henderson, in conversation with the author, September 2025.
3 Sun Tzu, *The Art of War* (London, 2023), p. 15.
4 Peter Payne, *Martial Arts: The Spiritual Dimension* (London, 1981), p. 5.
5 Norli García, 'Exploring the Spiritual Side of Martial Arts', *Whistlekick*, www.whistlekick.com, 29 July 2019.
6 Joe Hyams, *Zen in the Martial Arts* (New York, 1979), p. 19.
7 Kazumi Tabata, *Mind Power* (Tokyo, 1943), p. 15.
8 Stephen Turnbull, *Ninja: The True Story of Japan's Secret Warrior Cult* (Dorset, 1992), p. 9.
9 Paul Bowman, *The Invention of Martial Arts* (New York, 2021), pp. 100, 103.
10 Chris Crudelli, *The Way of the Warrior* (London, 2008), p. 210.
11 Christopher Springham, in conversation with the author, November 2024.
12 Yuji Yamada, 'The Spirit of Ninja' lecture, Mie University, www.human.mie-u.ac.jp, 1 October 2012.
13 Wouter Hanegraaff, *New Age Religion and Western Culture: Esotericism in the Mirror of Secular Thought* (Leiden, 1996), p. 10.

6 Forward Moves

1 Luke Archer, in conversation with the author, May 2025.
2 Charles Harris, in conversation with the author, May 2025.
3 Ibid.
4 José Ortega y Gasset, *Meditations on Quixote* (Madrid, 1914), p. 36.
5 Luke Archer, 'De-Escalate Conflict in just 12 Words', Association of Ki Aikido, https://akaikido.co.uk, 1 March 2024.
6 UNESCO, *Youth Development Through Martial Arts* (Paris, 2019), p. 12.
7 Saiorse Graber, in conversation with the author, April 2025.
8 Asier Cía, in conversation with the author, April 2025.
9 Charles Harris, conversation.
10 Luke Archer, conversation.
11 P. Douris et al., 'Fitness Levels of Middle Aged Martial Art Practitioners', *British Journal of Sports Medicine*, XXXVIII/2 (2004), pp. 143–7.
12 M. N. Zetaruk, 'Injuries in Martial Arts', *British Journal of Sports Medicine*, XXXIX/1 (2005), pp. 29–33.
13 Paul Abel, in conversation with the author, July 2025.
14 Daniel Powell, interviewed by the British Judo Association, www.britishjudo.org.uk, 14 May 2025.
15 Karen Roberts, in conversation with the author, July 2025.
16 Ray Sweeny, in conversation with the author, July 2025.
17 Ibid.
18 Carlos Gutiérrez García, in conversation with the author, July 2025.
19 Ibid.
20 Ibid.

SELECT BIBLIOGRAPHY

Adams, Frederick, and Gillian Webster, *Hands Off!* (Norwich, 1986)

Anslow, Stuart, *The Encyclopaedia of Taekwon-Do Patterns*, vol. I (London, 2010)

Barton-Wright, Edward William, *The Sherlock Holmes Book of Self-Defence*, reprint (Lewes, 2011)

Bennett, Alexander, *An Insider's Guide to the Japanese Martial Arts* (Rutland, VT, 2023)

Bowman, Paul, *The Invention of Martial Arts* (New York, 2021)

Catarevas, Eve Nadel, *Rena Glickman* (Minneapolis, MN, 2022)

Clark, Robert J., and Duk Sung Son, *Korean Karate: The Art of Tae Kwon Do* (Englewood Cliffs, NJ, 1968)

Cleary, Thomas, *Code of the Samurai* (North Clarendon, VT, 1999)

Clements, Jonathan, *A Brief History of the Martial Arts* (London, 2016)

Conan Doyle, Arthur, *The Complete Sherlock Holmes* (New York, 1987)

Corcoran, John, *The Martial Arts Companion* (New York, 1992)

Crudelli, Chris, *The Way of the Warrior* (London, 2008)

DeMarco, Michael A., ed., *Asian Martial Arts* (Santa Fe, NM, 2012)

Eggleton, Heidi, and Skea Derek, 'Women's Perceptions of How Martial Arts Influences Their Psychological Well-Being', *Martial Arts Studies*, 16 (December 2024), pp. 8–19

Faulks, Martin, *The Path of the Ninja* (London, 2015)

Fleming, Ian, *Goldfinger* [1959] (London, 2004)

García, Carlos Gutiérrez, *Judo* (Barcelona, 2011)

Geertz, Clifford, *The Interpretation of Cultures* (New York, 1973)

Gibson, Melanie D., *Kicking and Screaming: A Memoir of Madness and Martial Arts* (Berkeley, CA, 2021)

Gillis, Alex, *A Killing Art* (Toronto, 2011)

Godfrey, Emelyne, *Femininity, Crime and Self-Defence in Victorian Literature and Society* (London, 2012)
Green, Thomas A., ed., *Martial Arts of the World*, 2 vols (Santa Barbara, CA, 2001)
—, and Joseph R. Svinth, eds, *Martial Arts in the Modern World* (Westport, CT, 2003)
Griffiths, Andrew, *The Birth of the Samurai* (New York, 2019)
Haines, Bruce A., *Karate's History and Traditions* [1968] (Rutland, VT, 1997)
Hornsey, Kevin, *Taekwondo* (London, 2002)
Houseman, Robin, *Unleash the Lioness* (London, 1993)
Hyams, Joe, *Zen in the Martial Arts* (New York, 1979)
Lee, Bruce, and M. Uyehara, *Bruce Lee's Fighting Method* (Burbank, CA, 1977)
Lewis, Peter, *The Martial Arts* (London, 1996)
Lorge, Peter, *Chinese Martial Arts* (New York, 2012)
Meyers, Ric, Karen Palmer and Bill Palmer, *The Encyclopedia of Martial Arts Movies* (Columbia, MD, 1995)
Miller, Davis, *The Tao of Bruce Lee* (London, 2000)
Mitchell, David, *The New Official Martial Arts Handbook* (London, 1984)
Nicol, Clive William, *Moving Zen* (London, 1975)
O'Neil, Dennis, *The Dark Knight* (London, 2008)
Payne, Peter, *Martial Arts: The Spiritual Dimension* (London, 1981)
Pine, Red, trans., *The Zen Teaching of Bodhidharma* (London, 2019)
Pingyuan, Chen, *The Development of Martial Arts Fiction* (Cambridge, 2012)
Polly, Matthew, *Bruce Lee: A Life* (London, 2018)
Ratti, Oscar, and Adele Westbrook, *Secrets of the Samurai* (Rutland, VT, 1973)
Roosevelt, Theodore, *An Autobiography* (New York, 1913)
Rosenbaum, Michael, *The Fighting Arts: Their Evolution From Secret Societies to Modern Times* (Boston, MA, 2002)
Rouse, Wendy L., *The Origins of the Women's Self-Defense Movement* (New York, 2017)
Sonnon, Scott, *Mastering Sambo for Mixed Martial Arts* (New York, 2008)
Stewart, Rodney, *Mixed Martial Arts* (Melbourne, 2015)
Tabata, Kazumi, *Mind Power* (Tokyo, 1943)

Turnbull, Stephen, *Ninja: The True Story of Japan's Secret Warrior Cult* (Dorset, 1992)
Twigger, Robert, *Angry White Pyjamas* (London, 1997)
Tzu, Sun, *The Art of War* (London, 2023)
UNESCO, *Youth Development Through Martial Arts* (Paris, 2019)
Wile, D., 'Taijiquan and Daoism: From Religion to Martial Art and Martial Art to Religion', *Journal of Asian Martial Arts*, XVI/4 (2007), pp. 8–45
Zoughari, Kacem, *The Secret History of Ninjutsu* (North Clarendon, VT, 2010)

ACKNOWLEDGEMENTS

My gratitude, first and foremost, goes to taekwon-do Grandmaster Donato Nardizzi, for the years of instruction and guidance he has given me in my chosen martial art. Sixth Dan Alex Nardizzi is my current instructor, to whom I extend my thanks for the expert instruction that has hopefully instilled in me the self-confidence required to pursue this demanding practice.

Thanks are due to all the martial arts practitioners and historians whose knowledge has proved invaluable in writing this book: Keiron Henderson, Paul Bowman, Charles Harris, Luke Archer, Christopher Springham, Melanie D. Gibson, Master Shi Yan Gui, Daniel Beard, Myrsini Chionia Christodoulelli, Rachel Lockton, Mark Li, John Tasker, Carlos Gutiérrez García and Josiah Farrelly, with sincere apologies to any I have neglected to mention.

I am deeply grateful to the editorial team at Reaktion, especially commissioning editor Vivian Constantinopoulos, editor Emma Devlin and copyeditor Amy Salter. They are a delight to work with.

Lastly and as always, Helen Crisp's guidance has proved invaluable. Special thanks to my agent Duncan McAra, now retired, who has fought my corner throughout my literary endeavours.

PHOTO ACKNOWLEDGEMENTS

The author and publishers wish to express their thanks to the sources listed below for illustrative material and/or permission to reproduce it:

Alamy: p. 110 (Keystone Press); Myrsini Chionia Christodoulelli: p. 96; Asier Cía: p. 158; Ross Grabner: p. 157; Charles Harris: pp. 152, 153; iStock: pp. 9 (somethingway), 27 (wonry), 28 (bazzier), 42 (FG Trade), 45 (Jacob Wackerhausen), 46 (OSTILL), 59 (primipil), 117 (Gwengoat), 121 (Antonio_Diaz), 162 (Drazen Zigic); Library of Congress, Washington, DC: p. 106; Arthur Wallis Mills for *Punch*: p. 81; Alex Nardizzi: p. 14; Donato Nardizzi: p. 105; Shi Yan Gui: p. 6; Christopher Springham: p. 141; Wikimedia Commons: pp. 19 (photo Shi De Ru (Shawn Xiangyang Liu), CC BY-SA 3.0), 56 (photo President.az, CC BY-SA 4.0 International).

INDEX

Page numbers in *italics* refer to illustrations